"I have spent much of my life working with men and gifted leaders and teachers of men around the country. Brent Henderson and *Into the Wilds* have a special place in my heart. I love how Brent combines a terrific mix of hard-to-top guy stories from his professional hunting and adventure background, to the daily challenges men face every day. His humility is genuine and the dangerous truth he gives in this book are transformational and transferrable. In a world of great danger and great opportunity, this book will be a wise guide to help men navigate with courage and confidence."

—*Randy (RT) Phillips*
Former President, Promise Keepers
Men's Pastor, Life Austin Church, TX

"*Into the Wilds* reveals Brent Henderson's passion for helping men see where they have been snagged spiritually, and guiding them to the absolute joy of being set free from that bondage. This timely collection of stories of adventure and insight has the potential to change not just the man, but everyone else in his life."

—*Steve Chapman*
Author, *A Look at Life from a Deer Stand*

"I went on an amazing, once-in-a-lifetime trip to Alaska with Brent, along with my son. We stood within yards of eight-hundred-pound brown bears, filming them as they pulled salmon out of the Russian River. It was both exciting and a little scary at the same time. The danger was real. We listened to many of Brent's adventure stories around campfires, and we became part of some of his new stories. We had a gun, but more importantly, we had an experienced guide. *Into the Wilds* is tapping into that experienced guide. This is the 'dangerous truth' men need to hear. Read it and become moved and educated all at the same time."

—*Derek Daly*
Formula 1 and Indy car driver, best-selling author,
international racing champion

D0910919

"Brent and I have spent the last twenty years in the wilds hunting, hiking, and exploring. We have lived on the edge and encountered many things that would throw most men into panic mode. These same principles he teaches in *Into the Wilds*, I have been able to use in my corporate and business experiences in dealing with people, crisis, and challenges for successful outcomes. *Into the Wilds* will prepare you for whatever challenges life throws at you."

—*Brandon Jeffress*
President and founder, JumpSetter

"Discovering one's identity in Christ rather than in the idols of performance and other people's opinions is the most important issue facing men of the twenty-first century. Brent clearly communicates this transformative message in his book, *Into the Wilds*, through his masterful storytelling of real-life adventures. Dangerous. Life-changing. Truth."

—*Derek Wilder*
Executive Director, Lives Transforming Group, Inc.
Author, *Freedom: How Grace Transforms Your Life Now*

"Brent's courage to ask the hard questions is what makes him uniquely positioned to help men uncover the truth about God's design for their lives. In *Into the Wilds*, Brent borrows from his own unique experiences as an experienced outdoorsman. He utilizes the physical and spiritual lessons learned in unforgiving environments to create a survival blueprint that speaks to the real heart of men. Brent offers a spiritual strategy to not just brave the wild, but survive it and win."

—*Thomas Benge*
Retired police Sgt., tactical trainer, strength coach, speaker,
teaching pastor

"In the dictionary, under 'man's man,' you will find a picture of Brent Henderson. In *Into the Wilds*, Brent writes deftly to the heart of men, articulating the truths of grace and identity in Christ. The combination of those two abilities, woven together by God, make for a fascinating read and some excellent insight for a man's journey in Christ. *Into the Wilds* is unpolished and heroic all at once—just like the men he is reaching with this book."

—*John Lynch*
Author/Teaching Pastor, Open Door Fellowship, Phoenix, AZ

"Getting men to engage, especially when it comes to things around God, is a difficult task. Anyone who has worked in men's ministry for very long will tell you that. Brent Henderson understands the heart of a man—what makes him tick and how to get into his world. His ability to capture and hold a man's attention within the first sentence is truly a gift. In *Into the Wilds*, Brent takes us on an amazing journey from the wild forces of nature to the home front, where the forces of the enemy want to kill, steal, and destroy the heart of a man. Brent helps men to reclaim what the enemy has tried to steal…their identity."

—*Chris Mishler*
Vice President, MenMinistry.org

"Bombs were exploding. Debris was falling like rain. Men were yelling, blood was spilling, and my mind was spinning. Even though I was injured, I had to triage my patients in order to treat those with life threatening injuries first. How was I able to filter out the nonessential noise and prioritize the essential tasks? How was I able to do my job as a medic without losing my head or becoming paralyzed? The answer is easy: my training and my wingman. In the military, we learn, we train on what we learn, we fight the way we train, and our wingman has our back. Our Christian walk as men is much like combat in the desert. We need to train our minds to act without thinking. When sin pops up and our enemy comes to attack, we need to be so grounded in the Spirit as to automatically know what God wants us to do—then do it. When we fall, we need to have a loving, nurturing, nonjudgmental wingman who will come alongside us and help us get back on our feet. *Into the Wilds* will help you find your way through the dry spiritual desert that many of us have been trapped in. Study, learn, train on what you learn, and find a wingman to watch your back. Find the life God has designed for you—a life full of adventure, spiritual battles, and passion."

—*Ret. MSgt. Bruce Cooper*
Desert Storm, Operation Southern Watch, OIF 1, OEF 5&6 Q OIF

"As a former fighter pilot, and now an officer trusted to provide reliable force-structure advice to the highest levels of USAF leadership at the Pentagon, I can appreciate why Brent Henderson's book *Into the Wilds* is a must-read for men like me: first, when under attack, men needed to know they can defeat the enemy, or know they can survive and escape; second, as a Christian husband and father, *Into the Wilds* offers what no other men's book does—'how to' instructions for getting the job done. As a man called to serve my family, and who has made it my life's work to win at it, for their sake, I need help with the 'how' in the same way I needed a cadre of instructors to teach me how to fly, fight, and win in combat. If you're anything like me, you'll be awakened by Brent's book, and you will find the missing tools you need to live life the right way."

—*Dr. Kirk "Bubba" Horton*
Lt. Col., USAF (retired)

"Something is stalking the minds of men. It is the roar of a lion that re-verberates across miles. (See 1 Peter 5:8.) We have been told the threats are temptations of money, sex, and power. In the circles I walk as a pastor, danger lurks at a much more primal level. *Into the Wilds* is set in the adventure of God's wild creation, but the hunt takes us deep inside every man, to our very heart. Men are on a quest for identity. 'Who am I?' And, more significantly, 'Who am I in Christ?' Brent Henderson leads us to self-discover answers to these foundational questions. But this is not just a men's book. This is for anyone who is tracking deeper answers to their wandering hearts and lives. *Into the Wilds* is must-read!"

—*Pastor Keith Wooden*
Ovid Community Church, Anderson, IN

"Some authors write because they've spent time studying a subject in books. Other authors write because they've experienced what they're writing about. Brent Henderson is the second type. He has the experience! I know he does because I've been with him on many of his adventures. As a western big-game hunter, I can attest that Brent has the grit and gristle it takes to be a man's man! As a pastor, I connect with his heart for men and the biblical challenges he illuminates with clarity and truth. Men, it's time to read *Into the Wilds* and to step up to our responsibility of leadership for our kids. Brent's book will call you into the game!"

—*Roger K. Medley*
C-130 flight engineer, Air Force Special Operations
Founder, Backcountry Bowhunting

BRENT ALAN HENDERSON

INTO THE
WILDS

THE DANGEROUS TRUTH
EVERY MAN NEEDS TO KNOW

WHITAKER
HOUSE

Into the Wilds:
The Dangerous Truth Every Man Needs to Know

Menministry.org
Livestransforming.com

Lives Transforming Group, Inc.
433 E. 53rd St.
Anderson, IN 46013

ISBN: 978-1-64123-004-9
eBook ISBN: 978-1-62911-995-3
Printed in the United States of America
© 2018 by Lives Transforming Group, Inc.

Whitaker House
1030 Hunt Valley Circle
New Kensington, PA 15068
www.whitakerhouse.com

Library of Congress Cataloging-in-Publication Data (Pending)

1 2 3 4 5 6 7 8 9 10 11 ⊔⊔ 25 24 23 22 21 20 19 18

CONTENTS

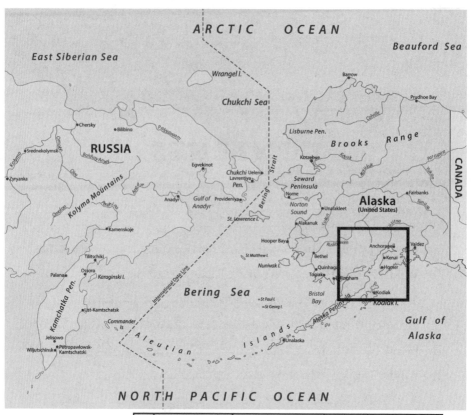

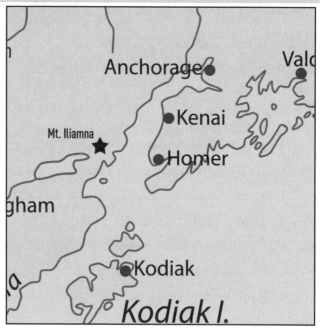

Mt. Iliamna

INTRODUCTION

MAYDAY:
MY FIRST TRIP INTO THE
ALASKAN WILDERNESS

(August, 1984)

The three of us had loaded our gear and packed a couple hundred pounds of caribou meat into the rear of a small plane. As we taxied across the Alaskan tundra and the pilot turned into the wind for takeoff, he quickly decelerated and announced, "Boys, we've got too much weight in the plane. We need a plan B." Our plane was overweight for such a short runway. Plan B involved removing our gear and flying me alone, along with several thirty-gallon trash bags of blood-coated caribou meat, to another spot some forty miles away. Then the pilot would return to pick up my friend Ralph and the rest of our gear. Since sudden weather changes could occur at our location at the drop of a hat, it was imperative that plan B went into effect immediately.

We had been on a caribou hunt in the Iliamna Mountain Range but the weather had turned miserable and we had become stranded for the past week. We made the best of it as we awaited the return of our bush pilot, who was flying with VFR (visual flight restrictions), not by instrumentation.

Flying VFR can be a death sentence for bush pilots as the fog and clouds can become so thick that they resemble a white, woolen blanket that drapes over your windshield, blinds the pilot, and can swallow a small plane without a trace. Alaskan bush pilots have a saying: "All the clouds have rocks in them." That's how easy it is to fly through a cloud and into the side of a mountain. Many of them learned that lesson the hard way.

Our pilot fit the bill of a stereotypical Alaskan bush pilot: large, unshaven, and loud, with a handshake that would crumple lesser men. These are rugged men, always living on the edge. They have nerves of steel, uncanny skills, and walk a fine line between genius and psychopath. They have years of experience navigating almost blind through the worst mountain weather Mother Nature can dish out. Alaska is breathtaking but extremely unforgiving. There's another saying bush pilots have: "Alaska's beautiful, but she's got teeth."

As we reached our plan B destination, the pilot circled the spongy tundra several times to make sure there was enough space to land. There were no runways, control towers or windsocks, only the skill of the pilot to judge the conditions and a sharp eye to look out for large rocks or small ravines that could bend landing gear or tear up one of the oversized tires. As the pilot decreased power and touched down, the plane bounced from side to side, eventually coming to rest on its tailwheel. Without shutting down the engine, the pilot passed me his AR-15, as I'd left my high-powered rifle at our other location. He pointed me to where he wanted me to mark off a new runway for his return, and told me to keep an eye out for bears.

During our approach, the pilot had pointed out a huge double-shovel caribou, limping along and trailed by a thousand-pound grizzly just waiting for the beast to topple over. I had always assumed that most large bears were sluggish and well-fed, like the ones we see at the zoo, but as we passed just thirty feet over this thousand-pound mass of teeth, claws, and muscle, you could see that this bear was wet, matted, muddy, hungry, and desperate.

As soon as the plane took off, I realized that I had failed to grab any extra ammo. I had one clip of .223 cartridges with the same external dimensions as the 5.56x45mm NATO military cartridge. Although a popular round, it's not the preferred line of defense you want against a large pred-ator that is bent on having red meat for dinner. About a minute after we took off and vanished from view, a staggering reality hit me: I was totally alone and there was an enemy nearby who could see my every move and determine if I was an easy target.

In truth, I *was* an easy target. I was a young guy, full of passion and desire for adventure, but I'd never been trained on how to survive in an environment like this. Few men have. I had very little of the "know-how" needed if things got bad—really bad. I had eight hundred dollars in useless traveler's checks tucked into my wallet, but I'd left my high-powered rifle back at camp. I can still see the pilot looking at me with a "Boy, where are you from?" look as he passed me his AR-15. His parting words still rang in my ears: "If the bear gets too close, just fire off a couple of rounds in its general direction and it should leave you alone."

I thought to myself, *SHOULD leave me alone?* My faith was strong and I knew how to pray, but in 1984, that was about the limit of my survival knowledge. I'd never fired an AR before and was too humiliated to ask for instructions—instructions that could save my life. Like so many young men, I had the hat and T-shirt but very little of the "know-how." I was clothed head to toe in the best outdoor attire money could buy, but I didn't ask for help because I was afraid of being exposed.

Starting to believe that the bear was more interested in a wounded caribou than it was in me, I began to explore the area. I ventured out about two hundred yards until I came to an incredibly steep rock face that ex-tended down from my position until it intersected with the ground floor some five hundred feet below. I remember thinking about how "all the clouds have rocks in them" and how I'd never want to be in a plane wreck up here because no one would ever find me. No sooner had that thought gone through my mind when I spotted something red and white on the rocks about seventy-five feet below me. There, smashed like a balsa-wood model, was a small plane. My stomach climbed up into my throat as I made my way to the wreckage, not knowing what or whom I might find. Looking inside, I discovered the plane to be empty of occupants and stripped of all electronics, but I couldn't imagine how someone could have survived that calamity.

After about two hours, I heard the welcome sound of the Super Cub returning to pick me up. After repacking to properly distribute the weight for takeoff, the pilot turned the plane around, throttled her up, and headed into the wind. I breathed a sigh of relief as he climbed to altitude and began to relive our adventure, shouting at each other over the deafening drone of the prop wash.

The flight was going smoothly. The weather was clear behind us and looked clear in front of us until we got about halfway through the mountain pass on the trek back to Anchorage. As the cloud cover above us began to drop, we were forced to fly lower and lower—2,000 feet, 1,500 feet, 1,000 feet. The pilot turned around and said, "Boys, start looking for a place to ditch the plane because there are no runways and this weather is forcing us down…quickly."

No runways? Surely there were fields. I'd been living in the "lower forty-eight" for the past twenty-three years, but nothing there could compare to this terrain. All I could see below us was the swift-moving whitewater of a glacial melt stream, surrounded by huge rocks and dense forest. The pilot got on his radio and issued a Mayday call. He understood the need for someone else to mark our location, because the odds were quickly stacking against us and we needed help. We waited but there was no radio response and the enveloping clouds were engulfing us in a sea of white, forcing us even lower—400 feet, 300 feet, 200 feet.

Just as the pilot was ready to risk landing on a rocky creek bed (better than flying into the clouds with rocks in them), a voice crackled across the radio. I don't remember the call sign or his exact words; I just remember that he told us about a small runway a couple of miles dead ahead.

The bad news: he said we weren't allowed to land there because it was private property.

The good news: our rough-and-rugged, half-crazed bush pilot said, "I don't care what you say, sweetheart! We're landing!"

The male voice on the other end of the radio, not too happy at being called "sweetheart," reluctantly guided us to their location.

"You're going to see a sharp bend in the creek bed below you, surrounded by a group of pines. The runway is just on the other side of the pines. Set her down as soon as you clear those pines...*sweetheart!*" That was the last communication we had before landing safe and sound.

There are times in life when even experienced bush pilots know to ask for help when they need a guide—and in this case, it saved our lives. Real-life storms, whether in the wilds or on the home front, have a way of forcing the level of your faith life and your know-how into the open. My faith life was strong, but I had very little of the "know-how" needed to survive. It was time for me to be willing to take the price tags off my clothing and get a little dirty. I needed more than just the wilderness hat and T-shirt. Like our pilot, I needed a guide to lead me through both the spiritual and physical wilds.

My Alaskan tundra plane and bush pilot.

SURVIVING THE HOME FRONT

If you think the strength of your faith and your repetitive prayers are all you need to survive in the wilderness matrix we'll call the "home front," you're either foolish, arrogant, self-righteous, or extremely naive.

Sometimes in life you feel like you are losing altitude and there is no one out there to hear your Mayday call. It feels like you've been stranded on a mountaintop all alone and searching for some sign of hope, but all you find is empty airplane wreckage stripped of every bit of its original existence. You've been left to the wilds, to the hungry bears and torrential downpours, and although you are wearing all of the new gear you were told you would need, you don't know where to turn next. Maybe you are a crack shot who can bring down a caribou at three hundred yards, but that kind of skill is of no use to you if you don't know how to clean it, pack it, or cook it so that it's actually useful to you. You've got the gear, you've got the guts, but you don't know how to use the guide. You need to be led and taught in life, a spiritual process called being *discipled*. And guess what? You can't do it alone.

Life is not formed on icy, ragged peaks; instead, it is nourished through the change of seasons. It is forged by winding rivers, pounding rain, and blowing winds. It is nourished and grown in the rich soil of deep valleys where relationships happen and new life begins. God knew the best view of a mountain would come from the valley floor. God desires a relationship with you and relationships for you.

This book is designed to take you from the mountain peaks to the ocean floor, and into the wild unknown. I want to help you to take the lessons and skills you've learned from the unpredictable wilds of nature and apply them to the home front, where we all live. As you read this book, the Holy Spirit will be your guide to help you discover the freedom of living a Christ-centered life. If you let Him, He will lead you on an amazing journey where you can finally break the chains of needing to perform for your worth. He will help you to escape the prison of other people's expectations and opinions. He will teach you how to uncover Satan's lies and destroy them with God's truth. You'll learn how to determine your spiritual temperature and how to acquire the tools needed to demolish unhealthy thoughts. You'll learn how to create safe environments in which trust can be built. You'll discover how life's challenges are truly gifts. In the end, you will find yourself equipped to make other disciples.

> *Two are better than one, because they have a good return for their labor: if either of them falls down, one can help the other up. But pity anyone who falls and has no one to help them up.* (Ecclesiastes 4:10)

PUSHING THROUGH

Listen, guys, I know how much it sucks trying to make friends in the church, and how much harder it is to help one another once you do make a friend. The church has failed to make the process of discipleship into something appealing, let alone exciting. Most of the time, you are expected to hang out with the guys who live near you or serve on the same committees as you do. If you are lucky enough to be married, you've definitely been forced to hang out with that guy on your church's basketball team who wears goggles and a sweatband, only because your wife has become best friends with his wife. Men hate forced friendships. What's even worse is when you finally make a buddy but all he talks about are his accomplishments, because his insecurity makes him constantly try to impress or "one-up" you. There's definitely a point where you want to say "bag it" and go back to hanging out with your old high school or college buddies and give up any quest for spiritual growth.

You have to push through. There *are* men out there who can help you grow when it comes to knowing God, and God will guide you to them if you'll just keep your line in the water. First you learn to survive in the wilderness, and then you become a guide to help others who are just as lost as you once were. I know that's a big leap—from feeling isolated and alienated from others to leading and discipling other men. Just like life in the wilds, it doesn't happen overnight. You first have to put in the work, gaining skill, experience, and wisdom, one excursion at a time. But I promise you, it will happen. First and foremost, *you will be set free!* Then, you will lead others in their quest for freedom.

JESUS, FISHER OF MEN

When it comes to leading and discipling other men, it's all about having the right gear and learning how to use it, and most of the time someone else needs to teach you. For example, using the correct hook when you are fishing can mean the difference between going home hungry or catching your fill. J-hooks had been used for decades to haul in every kind of fish known to man. But the change from J-hooks to circle hooks turned the commercial halibut fishing industry on its ear, causing such an increase in the long-line harvest in such a short time that scientists at first thought that the halibut population had exploded. No, there weren't suddenly more halibut, just a phenomenal increase in the effectiveness of the long-line fishery.

Once a halibut had a circle hook embedded where it belonged, there was little chance it was going to escape.

Hooking a halibut is a lot like discipling a man. How so? When you catch a fish, it's so that you can eat it. No, we don't want you eating anyone that you are trying to disciple (but if you do, let's not mention this book if anyone asks you where you got the idea). But you are trying to lure men in so that you can teach and lead them. Although you might find a fish or two on your own, knowing how to hook them, thereby giving you the ability to lead them, is a different story. Having the right gear—doing things like hosting men's events, being able to recite Bible verses, and quoting popular Christian songs—doesn't guarantee you a good catch. You have to know "where" and "how" to fish.

Jesus was called a "fisher of men." He knew where to go to find them, and He knew how to reach them. He didn't find them slouching in a church pew, half asleep. He went wherever they were and spent time with them, fished with them, went to parties with them, and then He asked them to follow Him. To catch a person who needs to be discipled, you've got to start thinking as they think and go to where they go, just like when you are fishing. Once you've got a good catch, it's time for you to learn how to lead, which is pretty much the same thing as discipling, so that your fish will learn how not to get caught by some other kind of lure later on in life. And believe me, there are some tempting, wooly buggers out there.

ARE YOU READY?

I encourage you to open your mind and your heart as you take a journey of your own through the spiritual wilds and allow yourself to be guided along the journey. Try to imagine yourself in a place where you are successfully applying the things you've learned in your own home front, a place where you have such faith in God's ability to disciple you that you can then reach out and disciple other men.

It's time for you to learn the dangerous truth every man needs to know as we journey *Into the Wilds!*

INTO THE WILDS GROUP STUDY FIELD GUIDE: WARNING! DON'T GO IT ALONE

"If either [man] falls down, one can help the other up. But pity anyone who falls and has no one to help them up."   (Ecclesiastes 4:10)

Y ou've got the gear, you've got the guts, but you don't know how to use the guide. You need to be discipled. And guess what? You can't do it alone. Life is not formed on icy ragged peaks, instead, it is nourished through the change of seasons, and forged through winding rivers, pounding rain, blowing winds, and grown in the rich soil of deep valleys, where relationships happen and new life begins. God knows that the best view of a mountain comes from the valley floor. God desires relationship with you, and relationships for you.

USING THE INTO THE WILDS FIELD GUIDE

1. FLYING SOLO

The *Into the Wilds* Field Guide is designed to be used on your own personal time, with a friend or a small group. I *highly* recommend reading *Into the Wilds* in its entirety before diving headfirst into the questions.

2. WITH A COPILOT

Another great way to utilize the *Into the Wilds* Field Guide is to take the journey through this paperback wilderness with a spiritual mentor or someone you trust. A copilot allows you to have someone to help you process the material, pray through it, and discuss what God is doing in and through you both. Always keep in mind that unconditional love and confidentiality is a key to building trust and encouraging spiritual growth.

3. WITH A CREW

Some of the deepest bonds between men occur while doing battle, sharing an adventure, or just having fun together. The effectiveness of this study relies on creating an environment of trust—an environment that draws everyone back each week. You might want to begin each week's session with a cookout, personal adventure stories, or an activity that keeps things fun and challenging. Completing the *Into the Wilds* Field Guide questions outside of the church building helps to create a more relaxed atmosphere, and decreases the pressure men may feel to "act religious." This allows for deeper and more honest interaction.

4. LANDING THE PLANE

At the end of each session, invite men to share how the chapter affected them, and whether the Holy Spirit revealed and "a-ha" or "take aways" moments to them. This will help them see truth more clearly, bringing revelation and encouragement to the group.

OPEN SHARE GUIDELINES

To be read by the group facilitator at the beginning of each session. The group facilitator will be responsible to maintain these guidelines and intervene whenever necessary to keep the group process safe.

1. CONFIDENTIALITY

What is said in group stays in group. We are encouraged to share our process with our support community, but we are not to share details or demographics of others' stories or identities beyond the group. While confidentiality is essential for healthy group function, there is a duty to warn others if an individual indicates intent to harm themselves or others.

2. SHARING

Keep sharing focused on yourself, not on others or their behavior. This helps to reinforce personal responsibility, as we can only change ourselves.

3. TIME

Keep individual sharing limited to 3–5 minutes. We all have important experiences to share and we want to allow time for everyone to participate.

4. NO CROSSTALK

We try not to "fix" or "feed" or interrupt others when they are sharing or interacting with the facilitator. This allows the Holy Spirit to speak to us individually as we listen to one another's journeys.

5. LANGUAGE

No graphic detail or offensive language that could be experienced as triggers by another man in the group (i.e., calories consumed, substances used, specifics of abuse, etc.).

6. NEW PERSONS

New members (first timers) are encouraged to share if they feel prompted. They should feel free to pass and not participate in discussions, as well. New members who share should focus on what brought them or what they experienced while hearing the teaching. The facilitator will thank them for coming and offer encouragement, but not offer guided discovery in the first encounter.

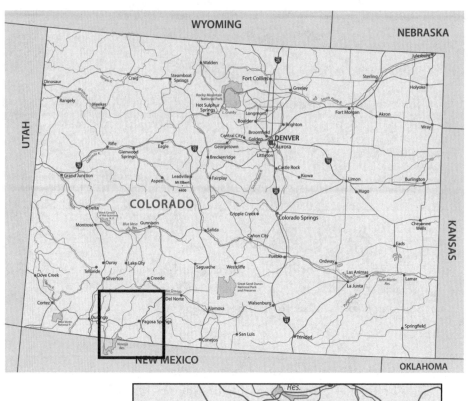

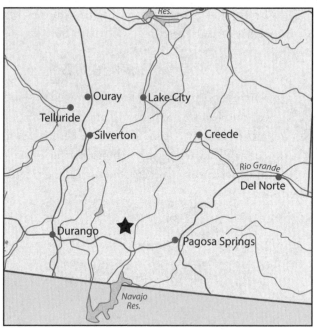

Poison Pass

THE WILDS

POISON PASS...DON'T WALK ALONE

It was mid-September in the Rocky Mountains of southwestern Colorado and the elk rut was about to swing into high gear. Three of us—Roger, Brian, and myself—had been bowhunting near Redstone for several days but decided to move to another part of the state as there had been too much pressure from other hunters. We needed to go deep and the going had to be rough enough to discourage other hunters from following in our tracks.

We arrived at the designated launching point overlooking Poison Pass early in the day to give us enough daylight to pack in our gear and set up a spike camp (a small camp consisting of two six-foot tarps stretched just wide enough to keep hunters dry if it rains) some five miles deep. We had intel that the bulls were bugling on the opposite side of the valley, but first we had to navigate through a canyon floor littered with trees thrown around like toothpicks and boulders tossed like giant Legos.

Checking my broadheads.

23

After sharpening our broadheads and sighting-in our bows, we cooked a quick lunch over a homemade, single-burner stove made out of a soup can, packed up enough supplies for several days, and began the long, steep trek down the mountainside. As we left the parking lot behind, the last thing we saw was a group of pack mules returning from a ten-day hunt loaded down with tents, stoves, sleeping bags, and the cape from a bull elk one of the hunters had taken. Our excitement level was rising!

My friend Roger bugling for elk in Poison Pass.

About a mile down the mountainside, we ran into a cowboy following up the original group. He was trying to locate a fallen muzzleloader one of the hunters lost on the way in. As we approached him, an extremely large and angry canine shot out from behind his horse, making a beeline for us, barking and exposing some nasty teeth. Caught off guard and a little surprised to see us, the cowboy pulled back on the reins of the horse, shouted "whoa boy," and then proceeded to call off his dog.

"Sorry fellas," he said. "We don't see much foot traffic in these parts." Those words should have made us question our decision to proceed any further into the bowels of the valley, but we were fixated on taking a nice bull.

After several hours of rough going over small streams, fallen logs, and enormous strewn boulders, we decided to take off our gear and do a little recon up the valley floor to see if any elk were still at the bottom before we moved any further through the canyon. The valley was surrounded on each side by steep canyon walls, walls we couldn't see because of the pines, aspens, tall grass, and thick foliage. It was a beautiful day, and stripping off our packs and doing a little forward scouting was a welcome break.

Thirty minutes into scouting the canyon floor, we uncovered a number of elk beds, two small six-foot wide streams, and a couple of cow elk mewing eighty yards in front of us. Rather than spooking the elk and blowing our chances of finding a big bull the following morning, we decided to pull back and set up a spike camp. After securing the ropes and stretching the tarp over our sleeping area, we unpacked our sleeping bags and bivy sacks (a small and extremely lightweight waterproof shelter used by climbers, mountaineers, backpackers, and soldiers). Then we grabbed some Mountain House meals and our homemade cooking stove and made our way about fifty yards away to the first of two small streams to make dinner. While finishing my last bite, I felt a small drop of water tap my nose, then another. We hadn't checked the weather radar after leaving Redstone, but didn't recall any hard rains being forecast for the area. Big mistake.

As I crawled into my sleeping bag and zipped the bivy sack around my face, the sporadic raindrops on the tarp above me, not more than a foot away, were mesmerizing and peaceful. About midnight, I was awakened by the crashing of thunder and flashes of lightning that lit up the canyon floor enough to see the water pouring off the leaves of the surrounding trees and ferns. By 2:00 a.m., I was roused from a sound sleep to discover that the thunder wasn't crashing anymore. Well, it's not that it wasn't still making a loud roar; it's that the roar was continuous. I had no idea at the time what I was hearing.

When I awoke again at first light, I could hear the rushing of water, and the rolling, continuous thunder felt almost feet away from my face. Like being shot out of a gun, the three of us immediately pulled ourselves out of our sleeping bags, only to be greeted by the sight of rushing water on both sides of us, just yards away! If we had done the math on the way in, we would have realized that all those downed trees and strewn boulders we saw were the result of not only the spring melt, but also the aftermath of strong storms that hit this canyon on a frequent basis. That's why the cowboy was so surprised to see us on foot in "these parts." We were in a canyon bottleneck where some of the stones probably served as grave markers to unsuspecting and naive pioneers and hunters in the westward push past the continental divide.

We were in real trouble. The two six-feet-wide streams we'd crossed on the way in were now raging rivers, and the rolling thunder was not thunder at all, but enormous boulders being rolled by the force of a current that would take out your legs and pull you under if you tried to cross on foot.

The rising flood waters that threatened to do us in.

We needed a plan, and we needed one now. Roger and Brian went downstream to try to find a crossing while I headed upstream. The entire trip was made by jumping boulder to boulder as that was the only high ground left. Within minutes of leaving the other men, the rains started to subside and I stripped off my outer rain gear (another mistake) to keep from sweating as I raced upstream. The temperature was in the low 40s, but I was sweating and didn't want to get soaked, as hypothermia can be a real killer if you get wet in cold weather with no way to heat up your body or put on dry clothes.

I laid my pack on the top of a large boulder, placed my rain suit next to it, unzipped the pack to take out a protein bar and continued upstream. After about a tenth of a mile crossing boulders and downed trees, the hardest rain of the entire trip unleashed itself like someone opening the tailgate of a dump truck full of water. Within seconds, I was soaked to the bone. The long johns I was wearing were so wet it was as if I'd jumped into a bathtub of water. I was in real trouble and I knew it.

Upon arriving back at my pack, I discovered that I'd forgotten to zip it back up after taking out the protein bar. Everything dry I had left was dry no more. I quickly re-zipped the pack, threw it on my back, and made my way downstream where I rejoined my friends at the place where the two streams, now rivers, converged. I didn't want to tell them about the dumb mistake I'd made by leaving my pack open and taking off my rain gear, but it didn't take long for them to figure it out as I was starting to shiver uncontrollably. Things were going downhill fast. At one point, I remember leaning over to unzip my pack, but I couldn't remember how to unzip it.

Just like in life, when bad things start getting worse, it's like an avalanche. If we didn't get ourselves out of there soon, it would cost us a life—not just one of us, but all three.

The next thing I remember hearing were the words of my friend, Roger, saying; "Brent, if we can't get out of here soon, we're going to have to get all those wet clothes off of you and put you between the two of us inside a sleeping bag."

One thing I do remember is what I said in response: "Um, we're getting out of here because that ain't going to happen!"

Roger and Brian took out one of the tarps we'd had over us in the night, pulled it over me, fired up the one-burner stove, made some hot cocoa and had me drink it to try to keep my core temperature from dropping below ninety-five degrees Fahrenheit. The warmth felt amazing as the steaming cocoa made its way through my body.

Some of the tarps I later used to restore my body temperature.

It didn't take long for the effects of the hot liquid to begin clearing my thoughts. Soon, the clouds also cleared, the sun pierced through, and the waterline on the rocks began to drop. As the sun hit the cool rocks, steam rose like incense, making a ghostly potion that moved across the waters and trees. For the next couple of hours, I dried my clothing by hanging them from a fallen tree, facing them into the sunlight.

It was time to move. Once I put on my "mostly dry" clothes, we began leaping from island to island, using small pines as bridges to cross the waters as they receded. After crossing approximately two hundred yards of low water, we could finally see dry land. It was a welcome sight! We hadn't gone more than a few hundred feet when we heard what sounded like jet engines up ahead. As we drew closer to the sound, we could see trees all bending in the same direction and shaking, almost as if an earthquake was happening. Our worst fears were becoming a reality fast. The water in front of us was worse than anything we'd seen behind us, by far. It was only about thirty feet wide, but it was a raging, brown torrent pulling in trees, mud, and anything in its path. There was no way around it.

DON'T GO IT ALONE

I'm reminded of a passage from James in *The Message* paraphrase that talks about how our faith life is forced into the open in times like these:

> *Consider it a sheer gift, friends, when tests and challenges come at you from all sides. You know that under pressure, your faith-life is forced into the open and shows its true colors.*   (James 1:2–3 MSG)

What you truly believe will come out. Knowing how dire the situation was, we began to pray, although silently (probably from exhaustion and in disbelief) that somehow God would deliver us. As if scripted by the best Hollywood movie ever made, we looked upstream, and there, hanging ten feet above the rapids, was a massive Ponderosa pine tree that had been uprooted by the force of the flood, and placed perfectly across the rapids. We couldn't do it on our own. This was the only way out. God had made a bridge.

How arrogant must we be to think we can navigate this world on our own? Maybe it's the images of superheroes like Captain America, Superman, or Wolverine, or the lone-wolf soldier images we've grown up with through action heroes like Sylvester Stallone, Dwayne "The Rock" Johnson, or Chuck Norris. Maybe a more realistic approach would be like the movies *Fury*, *The Expendables*, *Tombstone*, or *The Magnificent Seven*, in which it took a team of men, a band of brothers, to make it through difficult circumstances, each man relying on the strengths of the other men and showing up for each other when stuff hits the fan.

God had created a bridge that cold, wet day near Poison Pass, and He's built a bridge for us to live with Him in eternity through Jesus. It took a team of faithful men trusting God to help them navigate through the flooded Colorado wilderness, each using the skills and abilities their Creator gave them to fight their way through the wilds and back to the home front.

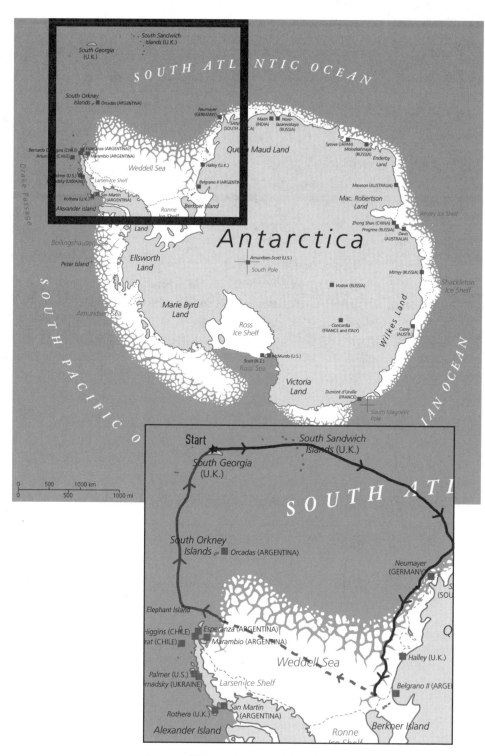

Imperial Trans-Antarctic Expedition

1

RISK DOING
SOMETHING DIFFERENT

"Difficulties are just things to overcome, after all."
—*Ernest Shackleton* | Polar explorer

One of the greatest stories of survival I have ever read is the story of the Imperial Trans-Antarctic Expedition, also known as the Endurance Expedition. It's considered the last major expedition of the Heroic Age of Antarctic Exploration. Born out of Sir Ernest Shackleton's imagination and his thirst for adventure, the expedition was an attempt to make the first land crossing of the Antarctic continent.

Shackleton's accomplishment as a leader started with his selection of a crew for this ship, *Endurance*. He handpicked some members, including two who had served him faithfully and performed exceptionally on a previous expedition. To recruit the rest, it is said that he posted the following notice about the difficult circumstances that awaited them:

Men wanted for hazardous journey. Small wages, bitter cold, long months of complete darkness, constant danger, safe return doubtful. Honour and recognition in case of success.

Shackleton's recruitment notice pulled no punches about the dangerous conditions their expedition would face. No member of the crew would be able to complain that they were not forewarned. These men were not an uncommon breed, as more than five thousand applied for this daring, larger-than-life, suicidal voyage! These were men who wanted to be a part of something bigger than themselves, and they understood that in order to accomplish this great adventure, they would endure weeks, months, and even years of discomfort. They were willing to leave the safety of the harbor because they understood harbors are not why ships are built.

On December 5, 1914, *Endurance* sailed from South Georgia Island for the Antarctic's Weddell Sea. As they moved southward toward Vahsel Bay, the ship encountered ice floes. Conditions gradually worsened until *Endurance* became completely frozen in pack ice on January 19, 1915. Despite months of frantic efforts by the crew to release her, the crushed ship sank on November 21, 1915, stranding her twenty-eight-man crew on the ice. Shackleton's calm demeanor was a steadying influence on his men in such dire circumstances. Alexander Macklin, the ship's doctor, said, "It was at this moment Shackleton showed one of his sparks of real greatness. He did not show the slightest disappointment. He told us simply and calmly that we would have to spend the winter in the pack."[1]

After months spent in makeshift camps as the ice continued its northward drift, the party took to the lifeboats on April 9, 1916, and endured five harrowing days at sea before reaching the inhospitable and uninhabited Elephant Island. It was the first time in 497 days that they stood on solid ground. Embracing reality that their chance of discovery there was unlikely, Shackleton made the difficult and dangerous choice of taking five of his twenty-eight-man crew on an eight-hundred-mile open-boat journey in the *James Caird* (one of their lifeboats) to reach South Georgia Island, which eventually led to the rescue of his entire crew and brought to an end their twenty-two-month expedition. Adversity drove these men to overcome unimaginable odds. Shackleton and his crew were saved because they embraced adversity, faced the dangerous truth of their circumstances, and were willing to risk doing something different.

REACHING AND LEADING REAL MEN

I speak at forty to fifty men's outreach events each year, put on by churches that are attempting to reach men who would not normally darken their doors. Most of these events have names like Wild Beast Feast or

---

1. Erik Seedhouse, *Survival and Sacrifice in Mars Exploration* (New York: Springer Praxis Books, 2015), xix.

Wild Game Dinner, but many of them are simply men's retreats. At each of these functions, the intent is to stir men's hearts with stories of wilderness adventures or hunting excursions and then, by the end of our time together, issuing an invitation into a relationship with Christ. Before each event, almost every church host tells me the same thing over the phone: "Brent, make sure to give them the Good News!" Unfortunately, many of these churches aren't prepared to know what to do with these men once the Good News has been shared and the event ends. Many of the men who run these churches have become too refined and lack the skills needed to take real men to the next level. It's like carrying a .338 Win mag into the wilderness but never taking the time to load the gun or practice how you'll handle things if a thousand-pound grizzly decides to chew on your ears.

Author and pastor Erwin Raphael McManus touches on this in his book *Unleashed: Release the Untamed Faith Within*. He writes,

> So what is this good news? The refined and civilized version goes something like this: Jesus died and rose from the dead so that you can live a life of endless comfort, security, and indulgence. But really this is a bit too developed. Usually it's more like this: if you'll simply confess that you're a sinner and believe in Jesus, you'll be saved from the torment of eternal hellfire, then go to heaven when you die. Either case results in our domestication. One holds out for life to begin in eternity, and the other makes a mockery out of life.[2]

The whole point McManus is making here is that we are speaking to men, talking about this great news, and ending the conversation by saying, "...and if you don't accept it, you'll burn in hell." Scaring men into a relationship with God is not "good news," as you can never truly love someone you're deathly afraid of. A woman may marry a man who puts a gun to her head, but that doesn't mean she's going to be *in love* with him. God wants to be in relationship with us, so much so that He died for it. The tragic truth is that only one out of every eighteen men, or 5.5 percent, have been taught to live a life full of Good News, and are then able to teach other men about it.[3]

2. Erwin Raphael McManus, *Unleashed* (Nashville, TN: Thomas Nelson, 2005), 32.
3. Patrick Morley, David Delk, Brett Clemmer, *No Man Left Behind* (Chicago: Moody Publishers, 2006), 134.

Brent speaks at a Wild Game Dinner.

This number includes not only the men sitting in church on Sunday mornings, but also pastors and church staff.

When speaking at men's events, I usually pose this question: "How many of you have ever really had another man coach you or teach you about God? I don't mean some religious class or accountability group. I mean man-to-man, authentic and real. The kind of real relationship that says, 'I know your *stuff* and I'm not judging or shaming you for it. I'll stick with you, no matter what, for as long as it takes!'"

When I talk about real relationships, I'm not talking about a man simply encouraging you to go to church, get baptized, join a small group, or pray more. I'm talking about finding a man who will teach you how to walk away when you want to lock your wife in a closet for a few hours, or how to hear the voice of God when you haven't had sex in six months. (I don't want you to hear His voice while you are having sex, because that would just be weird.) What I mean is hearing God and feeling contentment or peace about your world when you want to have sex with your wife but she is not interested. Hearing God when you are frustrated and tempted to find other outlets for those frustrations. Sometimes you just need someone to teach you to hear the Father's voice when He's speaking to you. Someone who can help you discern the Father's voice from the voices of enemies. Someone who can teach you how to fight off the lies of the enemy and how to apply and personalize Scripture to your life. Someone who will teach you to grow, share, and serve in your faith. Sometimes you just need someone else who is "safe" to talk to.

THE F-WORD

So why don't guys just talk to each other and help one another? When I was a young man, I felt inferior because of my (then) small size. Because of that I enrolled in a martial arts class and trained for years until I felt proficient enough to be able to handle myself if fighting became necessary. What I didn't learn was how to disarm conflict before fighting became necessary. I might be a black belt in the dojo, but I was a white belt when it came to conflict resolution. That's when I realized that I had a fear of failure.

Failure is one of the main ingredients that keep us from connecting with others and learning from one another within our spiritual lives. As men, we are deeply afraid of looking stupid, not tough enough, or not holy enough. Men don't like to do anything in which they might look stupid. They have bought into the lie that says they must have another man's respect in order to feel accepted. As long as a man is afraid he's going to look "less than," discipleship is simply not going to happen.

When men are part of a team with a coach, they accept the idea that the coach knows more than they do. They are comfortable with the idea that, hopefully, the coach will be able to teach them something to help them improve their game. In sports, you buy into the fact that you are less experienced than the coach in some areas and that he is going to help you in the long run.

In a discipling relationship, too often, men oppose one another to become "top dog" in the pack. In our fear of failure, we desperately want to avoid being seen as "less than" other men, so we flare our nostrils and stomp our hooves to take control of our territory. It's been that way for ages and it's not working anymore. It's time to realize that being a man of God means more than winning. It means that you are willing to take a chance on something else, to risk a little bit of failure in the hope of getting closer to God and one another, and, in turn, learning to live a better and more fulfilling life.

TRYING SOMETHING DIFFERENT WHEN THE OLD WAYS NO LONGER WORK

I know it's hard for guys to keep from having to prove that they are the best; it's part of our nature. Men want to fight fire with fire, but that's not how Jesus did things. Make no mistake about it, Jesus wasn't afraid of fighting for a worthy cause, but He picked His battles wisely, and without sin. How did He do this? First, He recognized that His battle was not with the rulers and authorities. His battle was against the true spiritual enemy:

Satan. He knew of Satan's ability to deceive others by casting darkness over their hearts and minds. Jesus knew that the real battlefield was being fought in the minds of men, and He was a master at winning this battle. His weapons weren't the typical weapons of warfare. He chose His Father's Word.

Jesus knew that truth, empathy, asking questions, telling stories, offering encouragement, bringing hope, and loving unconditionally were the ways to defeat the enemy. He didn't need others to like Him or accept what He had to say, because He knew that ultimately the truth would set them free. (See John 8:32.) The way He accomplished His mission was like no one in history had ever done it before. He didn't give in to the temptation of telling others what they wanted to hear for the sake of being popular. Jesus was not about being famous, but about laying down His own life—and in that, He was fearless. Through His death and resurrection, He gave us what we need to defeat the enemy's lies: His own identity. We will learn about our identity later, but for now, you have to understand that in order to get to that point, you have to learn to let go of the need to be "top dog" and your fear of looking "less than," and to embrace accepting help from your teammates. We all have the same goal! Learn how to get your gear working for you so that when you really do have to fight to survive, you will be ready.

Ernest Shackleton survived and his men were saved because he kept choosing to do something different. Sheer muscle couldn't break them free from the ice, withstand the negative-100-degree temperatures and 100-mph-winds, or survive countless dark, lonely nights. Hope is what saw them through, and that hope came through a leader they trusted to do whatever it took to find their way home. The captain of the *Endurance* was training his men how to take on harsh realities, confront fear, band together, and take calculated risks in order to survive the ruthless forces of a dangerous world. They had to do it together and teach one another exactly what doing that meant.

HITTING BOTTOM

One of my favorite survival movies is the film *Never Cry Wolf*, produced by Walt Disney in 1983. It was the inspiration for my first trip to Alaska in 1984. The movie dramatizes the fictional story of a government biologist/researcher sent to the Canadian tundra to research and collect evidence of the menace wolves were allegedly inflicting on caribou herds. The story begins with a pencil-pushing lab researcher named Tyler packing for a long journey to an unknown location deep in the Canadian arctic.

Having never been in a hostile environment, Tyler packs a veritable mountain of supplies that he "thinks" are essential inside the belly of a canvas canoe, including a pallet of toilet paper, several cases of light bulbs, boxes of government-issued carbon forms, and fifteen cases of beer. There's an old saying: "You can't fix stupid." Or, in the words of comedian Bill Engvall, talking about people who should carry signs announcing their stupidity, "Here's your sign!"

Tyler's preparations may seem funny and even a little ridiculous, especially to outdoorsmen, but even the best of us aren't much different. If you ask most men what they pack with them every day to navigate the home front, they'll probably say something like, "A rugged truck that has enough horsepower to pull a killer bass boat, a smartphone with 4G and Internet access, lots of man toys like golf clubs, bows, guns, camping gear, and jet skis, and a nice house with enough property for riding my four-wheeler." Then he'll say he needs a job that not only brings in a lot of money but gains the respect of other men around him. Oh yeah, and a beautiful wife hanging on his arm who makes him look and feel like a real man.

I'm not sure which one is more ridiculous: a geeky government researcher thinking he has what he needs to conquer the remote reaches of the Canadian tundra with a pallet of toilet paper and fifteen cases of beer, or the man who thinks that his identity is defined by how he looks, what he owns, or what he does for a living. Both men are living in a world where there is a silent, deadly enemy who wants to implant fear in men and rip out their hearts.

In the film, the world Tyler is about to enter is a world that even the most experienced trappers would shy away from. It's beyond remote, it's inhospitable, and it's deadly. Going into this environment alone and without extensive training in wilderness survival is not just foolish, it's a death sentence. Yet this is what most men do on a daily basis in this matrix we call the home front. We want to test ourselves to see if we have what it takes, only to discover that, after lost jobs, broken marriages, bruised egos, and crushed dreams, we need an experienced guide and a team of like-minded seasoned travelers who know how to navigate through this brick, steel, and concrete spiritual wilderness. Their fear of failure makes them not want anyone else to see them screw up. All of the extras a man uses to build himself up are just an elaborate mask he wears to avoid being exposed.

One of the most heart-pounding scenes in the movie comes when Tyler ventures onto a frozen lake while scouting for food. Not understanding that he's standing on thin ice, he proceeds to move forward. By the time he hears the ice begin to splinter and crack, it's too late. In the blink of an eye, he plunges into a cold, dark world where he cannot survive. The weight of his down clothing and excess gear pulls him down, his gut wrenching screams muted as he sinks to the bottom of this watery grave. He's drowning in a lake of inexperience and naiveté.

Above the surface, the wind blows and a light snow falls; life goes on as if nothing happened. No one can hear his cries. No one knows the fear and deadly cold depths he is sinking into. No one can come to his rescue. Tyler chose to go this journey alone and there was no one around to pull him to safety—a deadly mistake.

What saves Tyler? Hitting bottom. Only after hitting bottom is he able to strip off what he doesn't need and make his way to the surface, where he is able to use the barrel of his rifle to make a hole in the ice large enough for him to breathe air and eventually break through. Once free from the icy lake, he's still alone, naked, and inexperienced. In the coming days and weeks, things that go bump in the night will take over his thoughts inside the four walls of his survival tent.

Tyler has come face-to-face with the harshest environment on Earth, lacking the proper training and equipment. He looked the part, but underneath his brand-new name-brand gear, he was a pencil-pusher.

Today, Christ-following men often venture into the matrix of the home front having picked up the hat and T-shirt, just like I did, but very little of the "know-how." Like Tyler, most of us try to go it alone and survive in a hostile world that is both physical and spiritual. We need to take a lesson from Ernest Shackleton. We need to risk failure. We need to risk doing something different. We need to be discipled.

INTO THE WILDS FIELD GUIDE

CHAPTER ONE: RISK DOING SOMETHING DIFFERENT

1. When in your life have you been caught in a situation in which you were out of your element, and without the equipment or tools needed?

2. How did it make you feel?

3. As of a result of that experience, what actions did you take so that you wouldn't be "caught with your pants down" the next time?

4. Therefore, is having your weaknesses and/or inexperience exposed a good thing or a bad thing? Why?

5. What are some things in your world you believe you couldn't do without?

6. What types of things create fear for you? (For example, public speaking, starting a new job, finances, dating, talking to your wife, being asked to do something out of your element, etc.)

7. What's an area of your life in which you feel like you're standing on thin ice?

8. Would it be helpful to have another man to walk with you who knows you and is aware of your biggest fears and successes?

9. What could another man or group of men say or do to you that would *not* be beneficial in helping you walk through your deepest worries and fears?

10. What could another man or group of men say or do for you that would be beneficial in helping you walk through your deepest worries and fears?

Before a man can begin this journey through the spiritual wilderness, he needs to know he can't do it alone. He needs to have a safe place to process his thoughts and feelings without fear of being judged or condemned. This is key in creating a safe place that leads to life transformation, not merely conformity of behavior.

It's non-negotiable.

We *ALL* need a GUIDE.

We *ALL* need to be discipled.

"Christianity without discipleship
is always Christianity without Christ."
—*Dietrich Bonhoeffer*

2

WHO AM I...REALLY?

I n a Fox News segment, news anchor Dana Perrino interviews a US Navy SEAL discussing all the countries he has been deployed to.

She asks, "Did you have to learn several languages?"

"No ma'am," he replies. "We don't go there to talk."

Now it happened that while the crowd was pressing around Him and listening to the word of God, He was standing by the lake of Gennesaret; and He saw two boats lying at the edge of the lake; but the fishermen had gotten out of them and were washing their nets. And He got into one of the boats, which was Simon's, and asked him to put out a little way from the land. And He sat down and began teaching the people from the boat. When He had finished speaking, He said to Simon, "Put out into the deep water and let down your nets for a catch." Simon answered and said, "Master, we worked hard all night and caught nothing, but I will do as You say and let down the nets." When they had done this, they enclosed a great quantity of fish, and their nets began to break; so they signaled to their partners in the other boat for them to come and help them. And they came and filled both of the boats, so that they began to sink. But when Simon Peter saw that, he fell down at Jesus' feet, saying, "Go away from me Lord, for I am a sinful man!" For amazement had seized him and all his companions because of the catch of fish which they had taken; and so also were James and John, sons of Zebedee, who were partners with Simon. And Jesus said to Simon, "Do not fear, from now on you will be catching men." When they had brought their boats to land, they left everything and followed Him. (Luke 5:1–11 NASB)

Jesus never forced someone to follow Him; He merely invited them to join Him. The power of His life was such that it attracted men to follow. He was fully God and fully man. He understood the power of nature. He had created it. He also knew the power of a transformed life and what can happen when we cast our nets in the right place.

THE POWER OF A NAME

One of the most amazing displays of dedication, strength, and discipline I've ever witnessed occurred during a men's retreat in southeastern Pennsylvania in 2004. It was something that has stuck with me that I've shared countless times around campfires and while leading men's retreats.

All the men gathered for breakfast one late September morning after spending a fairly sleepless night in their sleeping bags, kept awake by the loud snoring of their bunkmates. As the men stood around waiting for the food line to open, nearly every all of them had a cup of coffee in their hand—second or third cups for many of them. There was very little discussion going on with this sleepy-eyed brigade. If they were honest, all they really wanted to do was go back to bed for another couple of hours.

After breakfast, the men sluggishly turned their chairs toward the front of the room as the retreat facilitator made a few logistical announcements and then began to introduce the morning speaker. Invigorated by a heavy dose of carbohydrates, protein, and caffeine, these men were now wide awake and their side conversations were almost drowning out the introduction of the presenter...until he got to the part that their speaker was a former Navy SEAL. Immediately, as if the men had a gun pointed to their heads, they stopped talking and an intense hush of deep respect washed over the room as each man gave his full attention. The SEAL walked to the middle of the room, and every man seated was awestruck. The SEAL had done nothing; he was simply introduced as a Navy SEAL. That's how much influence that title has on men.

SEALs command respect. They are the "best of the best." They understand their mission and are highly trained and motivated to get the job done, period. That morning, this SEAL's first words to the men were, "This is how the Air Force does pushups." Dropping to the floor, he began ripping off a series of slow pushups—down on four, up on four. He did enough that the average man's arms would have been shaking.

His next words were, "This is how the Army does pushups." He then began doing them with a clap in between each pushup.

"Next, this is how the Marines do pushups." He folded one arm behind his back and did ten one-armed pushups with each arm.

Smiling, he continued, "This is how the Coast Guard does pushups." He did these with his knees on the ground.

Finally, when no one else thought he could do anymore pushups, he spoke with determination: "This is how Navy SEALs do pushups." Instead of doing another variation of your typical pushups, he did a handstand in the middle of the floor without leaning against anything and began lowering his body down towards the floor until his nose touched the tiles. You could have heard a pin drop.

We later learned that he'd run eight miles before joining us for breakfast, only adding to the man's aura. While this superhero was conquering the world, the rest of us resembled a band of comatose morning zombies, mindlessly standing in front of the coffee pot, wiping the morning crud from our eyes, and attempting to stop dragging our knuckles on the ground as we tried to put sentences together that sounded like we had at least passed the second grade.

Later that afternoon, we were all instructed to get away and ask God who each of us really was to Him. We were told to ask God to give us a new name, just as Abram became Abraham, Saul became Paul, Sarai became Sarah, Jacob became Israel, and so on. One man came back saying he was God's "William Wallace"; another was God's "Maximus" (characters from the movies *Braveheart* and *Gladiator*). Others came back saying they hadn't heard anything from God about their new name.

I understand the point of getting away with God and asking the Father who we really are to Him, and although a name or a title like Navy SEAL may command respect, who we *really* are was never created from a cracked mold and can *never* be defined by an earthly title. We are shaped by our cracks, our flaws, and our sin, but the hands and the mold that holds us and formed us were forged in the heavens, created the universe, conquered death and sin, and crushed the head of the enemy. Each of our molds was created uniquely for us, with our name boldly and lovingly inscribed on it. It doesn't matter what other guys call you or what medals or trophies you've earned; they don't impress God or cause Him to love and respect you any more or less. His love is unconditional for those He calls His children, and when He calls our name, He's calling His own to Himself.

When we give power to any other name but "Jesus," we've given lesser names the power to define us and shape our thoughts, emotions, and actions. That may work for you on a good day when everyone wants to be you, but on days when we screw up, fall down, or betray, abandon, and murder with our words and actions, that name can take on a whole new meaning. And it happens to all of us. If you find a dude out there who tells you that he's never made a mess of something, then that guy is probably living in a mess bigger than anything you've seen. We all screw up, but lucky for us as believers, we bear the name of Jesus Christ, and that name can never lose its power, respect, and authority.

IT'S NOT ABOUT YOUR EFFORT

Several years ago, I spoke at a men's event near a naval base and I shared a story that was very close to my heart and I explained why. After the event, a large, muscled, tough-looking man approached me at the back of the auditorium. As he drew near, the men around me parted like the Red Sea to let him through. His right hand was clenched into a fist, making the veins in his enormous forearms pop out like a garden hose. As he raised his shaved head, our eyes met. What happened next was not at all what I expected. Standing by his side was his ten-year-old son, as streams of tears poured down the man's chiseled cheeks. For fifteen seconds, he tried to speak but no sound came out. Then, one word at a time, he began to put a sentence together.

"For thirteen years, I've been a Navy SEAL," he stammered. "I've tried to prove who I am by how I looked on the outside and by how many medals I earned and how many missions I completed. I fed off of the respect of others. When I looked in the mirror, that's all I could see...what's on the outside. Tonight, you said that it's who you are, not what a man says or does that makes him who he really is. You said that God doesn't keep a record of my sins when I belong to Him and that I'm defined by 'Christ in me,' not by my performance or what other people think of me. I've almost destroyed my marriage and kids from my need to perform at such a high level. Tonight, I received Christ as Lord and Savior of my life. I want to be a man who's not defined by my medals and mystique, but by who I really am on the inside."

As the man opened his huge clenched fist, the light revealed a golden Trident pin worn only by Navy SEALs. He placed the prestigious pin in my hand and told me to give it to my son and to make sure he understood that becoming a Navy SEAL doesn't make him a man. It's who he is on the inside that makes him a man. It's seeing yourself the way God sees you that makes you complete.

Then he said these words: "When people feel like somebody and then go back to being anybody, they end up feeling like nobody."

This man's transformation rocked the world of every man who heard him that night. The nets had been cast and drawn, and this strongman realized that he could not fight alone. He had been caught by Jesus' love and grace. He'd been made righteous through the blood of Christ, not by his own efforts. This SEAL was trading his trophies for transformation. He was learning who he was apart from being a Navy SEAL, apart from being a soldier, and apart from being a father. It was who he truly was in Christ that made him feel more than a nobody.

Read the following verse:

This righteousness is given through faith in Jesus Christ to all who believe. There is no difference between Jew and Gentile, for all have sinned and fall short of the glory of God, and all are justified freely by his grace through the redemption that came by Christ Jesus.

(Romans 3:22–24)

Look closely at this verse: *"This righteousness that was given through faith."* What does it mean to be righteous? Here is the definition of "Righteousness" from the *Baker's Evangelical Dictionary of Biblical Theology*:

God the Father is righteous (just); Jesus Christ his Son is the Righteous (Just) One; the Father through the Son and in the Spirit gives the gift of righteousness (justice) to repentant sinners for salvation; such believing sinners are declared righteous (just) by the Father through the Son, are made righteous (just) by the Holy Spirit working in them.[4]

Imagine if this elite warrior really understood where his true identity came from; not from being the "best of the best" but from the fact that God's best—His righteousness—is already in him! Imagine what, or whose, reflection he'd see when he looked in the mirror and how that might change his ability to lead and mentor his son and love his wife!

What about you? What are the medals you wear for everyone to see? Your job title? Is it the car you drive, the house own, the money in your bank account, or the trophy wife hanging off your arm? How would you feel if any of those things were gone tomorrow morning? Would you feel like a "nobody"? Where is your identity rooted?

As a child, I didn't know I was righteous because of God in me. Instead I saw myself as a skinny, near-sighted kid growing up in Northwest Pennsylvania. I was pushed around a lot. I believed what others said about me and I couldn't see myself for who I truly was. Those years were filled with life's most difficult lessons. At about the age of eleven, my grades began to drop from As and Bs to Cs and Ds. An eye exam revealed the problem. I had been moved to the back row of the class simply because of alphabetical seating arrangements and could no longer see the blackboard at the front of the classroom. Not being able to see, I soon lost interest and began daydreaming of sailing off to foreign lands, and my grades dropped below C level.

The shame of bringing home a bad report card paralyzed me, and I hid it from my parents until the day I had to return it, signed by my parents to let the teacher know I'd revealed my failure. Later that afternoon, my mother had a meeting with the elementary school teacher, and the result was an eye appointment with an optometrist the following day.

---

4. http://www.biblestudytools.com/dictionaries/bakers-evangelical-dictionary/righteousness.html.

Two weeks later, my glasses arrived. The very moment I put them on, I began to see things I'd never seen before. My mother still tells the story of the first time I walked outside wearing the new glasses. My first words were, "Mom, the trees have leaves on them!"

I simply couldn't see the real world because I didn't have the correct lenses. The reason I saw myself as a skinny, near-sighted kid was because I was looking through the world's lens. It wouldn't be for another thirty-five years and a devastating personal shipwreck that I would look at myself through Jesus' lens and see the real me.

So, who are we...really? What does this life in Christ look like under the Jesus lens? Paul summed this up in Romans 8 when he said,

> *Those who are in the realm of the flesh cannot please God. You, however, are not in the realm of the flesh but are in the realm of the Spirit, if indeed the Spirit of God lives in you. And if anyone does not have the Spirit of Christ, they do not belong to Christ. But if Christ is in you, then even though your body is subject to death because of sin, the Spirit gives life because of righteousness. And if the Spirit of him who raised Jesus from the dead is living in you, he who raised Christ from the dead will also give life to your mortal bodies because of his Spirit who lives in you. Therefore, brothers and sisters, we have an obligation—but it is not to the flesh, to live according to it. For if you live according to the flesh, you will die; but if by the Spirit you put to death the misdeeds of the body, you will live.* (Romans 8:8–13)

I recently did a radio interview where I was asked who my biblical heroes of the faith were. Peter tops that list. Not just because he was a fisherman, but because he had flaws. He was known to doubt, lie, and lash out in anger. He desired to be greater than others (performance issues), betrayed Christ, and yet he got back up time and time again to follow Jesus. Peter's life transformed from a man who hit rock bottom to a disciple, the man Jesus would eventually call "the Rock" and the one on whom He'd build his church. (See Matthew 16:18.) Peter's "hitting bottom" would begin the process of transforming him from sinner to saint, and not because of anything Peter did on his own, but because of grace alone. I am Peter.

It took me a long time to get to that point. Years ago, I had no idea who I was. My world was defined by other people's definitions of me. I listened to everyone else's ideas of who I was and never once thought that I needed to figure that out on my own. So much so that I ended up in therapy for it.

HI, MY NAME'S BRENT AND I'M ADDICTED TO APPROVAL

"Hi, Brent. Welcome to Celebrate Recovery. My name is Bill. What brings you here tonight? Alcohol addiction, drug addiction, sexual addiction, food addiction, codependency? A lot of people come here who've been trying to drown their sorrows, but we know those sorrows teach us how to swim!"

Those were the first words I heard as I walked in the back door of a church I'd traveled two hours to get to so I could secretly attend their 12-step recovery program. I'd driven that far because I didn't want anyone from my hometown knowing my issues. Like Peter, I was ashamed of who I thought I was.

My drug of choice was the approval of others. I responded to Bill's question with a hushed, "Um, I think I have an approval addiction."

"Never heard it called that," was Bill's response, "but I think maybe you might find help in our codependency group. Come with me after we do announcements and the serenity prayer and I'll show you where that group meets."

Why was I here? How did I get here? How do I get out of here? These were some of my thoughts that evening, but as the group opened up and began revealing their struggles, I knew I wasn't the only one in the room with this issue and there was some comfort in that.

MY MUSICAL IDENTITY

In 1982, I was touring with a band called The Chapman/Henderson Band. The original three group members consisted of myself, Herb Chapman, and his brother Steve Chapman (later to be known as Steven Curtis Chapman). We did two US tours and were starting to get a lot of attention. It felt good. I was not a popular kid growing up and to "be somebody" gave me a sense of worth. I was someone special, unique, set apart.

In 1984, we disbanded when Steven decided to move to Nashville to pursue a songwriting career. Afraid that I'd lose college credits, I chose not to make the move.

For the next year, I was still recognized as the Henderson half of the band and was feeling pretty good about myself. It opened some doors in the local studios and got me a few dates with the girls on campus, but as time went on, my self-worth diminished and I started feeling like just another guy on campus.

Two years later, I became part of another three-man vocal band called One. Within two months of forming the group, we were asked to accompany Sandi Patti on her world tour. One also

Members of Chapman Henderson:
(l to r) Herb Chapman, Steven Curtis Chapman,
Brent Henderson

scored a major record deal with Word Records and for the next five years, I was feeling on top of the world. We were no longer performing in front of crowds of hundreds; now there were thousands of people filling the seats to see us! Radio City Music Hall, *The Tonight Show*, *Nashville Now*, the Fox Theater, we were getting to do it all...and the addiction grew.

In 1992, my world came crashing down. One disbanded, Sandi Patti went through a painful divorce, and I found myself once again going from being "somebody" back to being "anybody."

For the next several years, I got my worth from being a studio singer, and in 1997, I got a solo recording contract. By January 1998, I was touring with Dove Award-winners Avalon and Crystal Lewis. My first radio single, "No One Speaks Your Name Like Jesus," quickly rose to number one on the music charts and my self-worth was once again on the rise. My identity was connected to radio charts, riding on a tour bus, people's applause, and how many fans wanted my autograph.

Performing on stage with Sandi Patti.

My last major concert appearance was on July 10, 1998. Strangely enough, I was asked to open for Steven Curtis Chapman at an event in Traverse City, Michigan. I remember sitting on the tour bus with him after the show and thinking, *Well, this is it. It's time to go back to being just anybody again.*

With the birth of our second child only three days later, I decided that I needed to get off the road, and pour myself into being a better husband and father. Maybe that was where my real worth would come from. After all, I'd achieved what a lot of people dream about. What I found out was that those types of dreams are not rooted in reality and when you wake up, if you don't know who you really are, those dreams soon become nightmares.

It wasn't long until the feelings of worthlessness began creeping back in. In 2002, my family moved to another state, and I took the position of worship leader in a fast-growing seeker-type church. The church grew from around 250 to 1,300 over the next four years, but this time, things were different. Instead of my new position filling the void of my "self-worth tank," I began to feel something different. I felt like who I was inside was being sucked out of me. I went from feeling like somebody back to being anybody, and eventually feeling like nobody.

Church work is not easy, especially if you don't have a solid sense of who you really are in Christ. People who are trying to get their own self-worth tanks filled will take every ounce of emotional gas you have if you allow them. If your tank is already empty, you will eventually find yourself trying to fill that tank through the respect and good opinion of other people. I would quietly hold up all of my past accomplishments: world concert tours with top artists, songs I'd written, commercials I'd sung, gold records, top-ten hits. I wanted others to see my trophies so I'd gain their respect. During those years, I learned something really ugly about myself. I had the ability to manipulate the opinions of other people to get my emotional needs met. I did whatever it took to feel better about myself, no matter who it hurt.

My unhealthy thinking—believing others' good opinions could make me feel better or worse about myself—caused me to hit the bottom. I call it my own personal shipwreck. My marriage was struggling and I bought into the lie that my wife should be able to meet my emotional needs. When those hidden expectations weren't met, I bought into another lie the enemy was whispering in my ear: "You deserve to be treated better." That lie almost cost me my marriage and hurt a number of other people. I ended up making the poor choice of getting too close emotionally to a woman I was working with.

Even though this emotional relationship was never carried outside of the workplace, it was sin. Like Peter, I doubted, I lied, and I lashed out in anger. I wanted to be greater than others (performance issues) and I betrayed Christ by my actions. I was being sucked down again, and instead of having someone there to reach into the dark waters to pull me free, many of those who were closest to me turned and quietly walked away. Their silence was deafening and I allowed others' shaming and condemnation to affect me. It became an anvil around my neck that was pulling me under. I could no longer keep my head above water. I was drowning. Jesus would have to pull me out of the raging waters once again.

> *Afterward Jesus appeared again to his disciples, by the Sea of Galilee. It happened this way: Simon Peter, Thomas (also known as Didymus), Nathanael from Cana in Galilee, the sons of Zebedee, and two other disciples were together. "I'm going out to fish," Simon Peter told them, and they said, "We'll go with you." So they went out and got into the boat, but that night they caught nothing.*
>
> *Early in the morning, Jesus stood on the shore, but the disciples did not realize that it was Jesus.*
>
> *He called out to them, "Friends, haven't you any fish?"*
>
> *"No," they answered.*
>
> *He said, "Throw your net on the right side of the boat and you will find some." When they did, they were unable to haul the net in because of the large number of fish.*

Then the disciple whom Jesus loved said to Peter, "It is the Lord!"
As soon as Simon Peter heard him say, "It is the Lord," he wrapped his
outer garment around him (for he had taken it off) and jumped into
the water. The other disciples followed in the boat, towing the net full
of fish, for they were not far from shore, about a hundred yards. When
they landed, they saw a fire of burning coals there with fish on it, and
some bread.

Jesus said to them, "Bring some of the fish you have just caught." So
Simon Peter climbed back into the boat and dragged the net ashore. It
was full of large fish, but even with so many the net was not torn. Jesus
said to them, "Come and have breakfast." None of the disciples dared
ask him, "Who are you?" They knew it was the Lord. Jesus came, took
the bread and gave it to them, and did the same with the fish. This was
now the third time Jesus appeared to his disciples after he was raised
from the dead.

When they had finished eating, Jesus said to Simon Peter, "Simon
son of John, do you love me more than these?"

"Yes, Lord," he said, "you know that I love you."

Jesus said, "Feed my lambs."

Again Jesus said, "Simon son of John, do you love me?"

He answered, "Yes, Lord, you know that I love you."

Jesus said, "Take care of my sheep."

The third time he said to him, "Simon son of John, do you love me?"

Peter was hurt because Jesus asked him the third time, "Do you love
me?" He said, "Lord, you know all things; you know that I love you."

Jesus said, "Feed my sheep. Very truly I tell you, when you were
younger you dressed yourself and went where you wanted; but when
you are old you will stretch out your hands, and someone else will dress
you and lead you where you do not want to go." Jesus said this to indi-
cate the kind of death by which Peter would glorify God. Then he said
to him, "Follow me!"   (John 21:1–19)

This made no sense to me. Why would God want me to follow? It was too late for me. I was a mess and there was no way that anyone was ever going to respect me or my opinion ever again. I had screwed up enough to ruin things for everyone in my life and I assumed that God would never want me working for him again. So why follow?

PARTING WITH PENNSYLVANIA

The fallout from my poor choice didn't look like a nuclear bomb blast, but more like a dirty bomb; it just lingered in the air doing more damage, a little at a time. The ugliness of my unhealthy thoughts, emotions and actions filled me with almost unbearable shame. My credentials weren't taken away or frozen, but my sin was brought before the staff, the leadership team, and the head of the state clergy health committee. My wife and I were sent to extensive out-of-state counseling, local counseling, required to complete a three-month financial course (in case that was source of our marital problems), and to attend and complete a 12-step recovery program. Finally, my wife and I were paraded (I don't believe paraded was the intent, but that's what it looked and felt like) in front of three back-to-back church services in which I read a shameful letter and confessed my sin to the congregation. During this time, the congregation was instructed not to call us or come to our house, as the church leadership felt that we needed to be separated from the church body in order to heal. In the months that followed, I never felt more alone or abandoned in my life. Their silence spoke volumes. If this is what restoration looked like, it was too much to bear.

At the completion of fulfilling those requirements, I was to then be reinstated into a part-time, not full-time, position on the church staff again. I fulfilled all of the requirements set forth, and, after confessing to the congregation, gave my letter of resignation to the church leadership. I was broken and humiliated and the strain was too much for my family. It was time to leave.

Several months later, our house was for sale. The church was kind enough to pay me for the several months and extend my health insurance as well, but the damage was done. Shame is a silent killer.

I moved my wife and children to the state of Indiana, and then returned to Pennsylvania to complete all the packing, painting, and repairs needed. That took me almost two months to complete. Most of my days were spent lying in bed unable to move, drowning in tears of shame and condemnation. I wanted to die. This is not what restoration should look like. I desperately needed to see myself through Jesus' eyes.

One evening, while still living alone at the old house, I was driving the hour and forty minutes home from the Celebrate Recovery program I'd been attending and listening to a Christian radio show. The speaker was Tony Evans, and he was talking about how what we have done in our lives does not define who we are. Tears began pouring down my face. Could that really be true? This isn't what had been communicated to me since my sin.

Needing to get everything completed at the house so I could get back to my family, my elderly parents were spending night and day helping me paint, repair a rotting deck, washing walls, packing boxes, and moving furniture, including a heavy antique piano. My father has always been a hard worker, but he wasn't a young man anymore. They returned home and a team of close friends showed up to help paint my daughter's bedroom later that afternoon. I was outside doing some painting when someone ran outside with the phone.

"Brent, your father has had a massive heart attack. They don't think he's going to make it."

Was this because of my sin, I thought? Was God stripping me of my family now? I ran inside the house, grabbed my keys, and followed a friend thirty miles to the emergency room. The trip took us twenty minutes. When I arrived at the emergency room doors, my elderly mother was waiting for me, confused, pacing the floor, and saying, "Brent, what will I do if your father dies?"

The doctor allowed us to enter the room where my father was being treated. His face was white as a sheet. Both his face and body were twisting from the excruciating pain he was enduring. They were prepping him to be flown to Pittsburgh by LifeFlight helicopter. This couldn't be happening. Not now! I needed his love and support. I didn't want him going out while I was going under. I wanted him to be proud of his son.

We heard the thumping of the helicopter blades overhead and the family gathered around him. He'd been throwing up and moaning in pain. In those last seconds before they came to get him, he looked at me and said, "I love you and I'm so proud of the man you are."

I kissed him, told him I loved him, and, moments later, he disappeared into the night sky.

He had suffered a massive heart attack that destroyed half of his heart. Several days after his release, I was back at home packing the moving truck. It was one of the hardest days of my life. I will never forget the three men and their sons who pulled into my driveway that day to help me load the truck and lock the front door for the last time. They didn't care about my past sin; they cared about me. They weren't on the church staff. They were Godly men who served a vital role in our men's ministry. They were leaders. These men had my back.

When the first man walked up to me as I was attempting to load the truck myself, his first words were, "Bro, this 'leave Brent and his family alone to heal' stuff is pure $&!#. We don't care what anybody else says; we love you and we're here to help. Give me a box!"

These men and I had fought against the enemy together, laughed together, cried together, and prayed together. We had shared life together. These were men I'd had the honor of discipling—faithful men of strength and honor, true to their Father in heaven. We had been a band of brothers. When the bullets started flying, they showed up, scaled the walls, and charged the gates of hell in order to come to my rescue. These powerful men threw off the garment of other peoples' opinions, held up the shield of faith, took up the sword of the Spirit, and did battle for me. Me! They weren't going to let me do this alone.

Our parting words were, "Strength and honor."

With tears flowing down our faces, it was time. I turned the key, put the truck in drive, pointed it forward, and pulled out of our driveway for the last time, leaving behind the people and community I loved.

Sin sucks.

God is good.

Soon, I was in Indiana and ready for a new start. My outlook was a little better, but I still wasn't ready to start hugging a bunch of guys and exposing the dark closets of my life. I had a long way to go.

ENTERING INDIANA

I'd only been in Indiana for about two weeks when a close friend invited me to attend a small group meeting near Indianapolis. At first I was reluctant as I didn't want anything to do with church. I wasn't eager to get close to anyone. I had convinced myself that I was going to do this alone. I didn't need anyone else. I'd tried that approach and they all abandoned me, except for a select few. I didn't want another accountability partner. My friend assured me that this was much different from church as we'd known it. So that night at 6:00 p.m., he picked me up and we headed to the leader's house.

At the end of the night's meeting, my friend asked the leader if he could find a few minutes to speak with me. We sat on the couch in his basement and, with a breath the size of Texas, I let out all of my sin for him to hear. His response: "I'm so sorry you and your family have gone through such a difficult time. It sounds like you've been trying to take steps to get healthy. Let's get together again next week and talk."

Really? That was it? No statements like "Well, that's the consequences of your sin" or "I've got another list for you to complete if you really want to be restored." He didn't use the infamous "I have an accountability partner I want to set you up with so this doesn't happen again."

The next week, we repeated the cycle. Meet for group, then stay and talk with him afterwards. This time, we moved to the couch upstairs. As we started talking, I started spewing again about how sorry I was for what had happened, how much I missed the people back at my former church, and how I felt like I still wanted to be in ministry.

I followed that sentence up with, "But I know I shouldn't be in ministry."

Again, his response jolted me. "Why do you think you still can't be in ministry?"

Don't you get it? I sinned!

"Brent," he said smiling, "there's something I want you to know. Christ's command to 'follow Him' wasn't and isn't dependent on your sin or lack thereof. God doesn't call the equipped; He equips the called. Nothing has changed your calling to be His disciple and to make other disciples.

"Brent, First Thessalonians 5:23 teaches us that we're made up of three parts: body, soul, and spirit. But the only eternal part is your spirit, and that's God's Spirit in your spirit. That's who you really are."

God wants you to know who you really are and who He really is! He wants to be by your side and He will not abandon you, no matter what you've done, are doing, or will do in the future. You are His. Your most difficult circumstances are transforming you into the man God desires you to be. Your true identity is *in Christ*!

INTO THE WILDS FIELD GUIDE

CHAPTER TWO: WHO AM I...REALLY?

1. Has anyone ever called you a derogatory name? If so, how did it make you feel and how did you respond?

2. If you really understood that your worth and value comes from God and not from others, would their "put downs" and disrespectful comments have the same effect on you?

3. If your answer to the above question was yes, what does that mean about where you're getting your worth and value from? If your answer was no, would it have affected you as much, and how might you have responded differently to their name calling?

4. Describe your first car. Was it something you were embarrassed by or did it make you feel better about yourself?

5. Did you do anything to that car to alter its performance or looks to attract attention or to impress your friends?

6. Who or what did you want to be when you grew up?

7. Did you become who you wanted to be? If not, why not?

8. What happens when we need others' good opinions of us to feel better about ourselves? What does that say about where you believe your righteousness comes from?

9. If you understood that there's nothing you could say or do that could make God love you more, and nothing you could say or do that would make God love you less, in what area of life would that affect you the most?

10. If you no longer had to live in fear about how others think of you, what would you do differently with your life?

Before a man can go deeper into the wilds, he must understand where his "good enough" comes from. Discuss the following verse and what it means to be righteous and why that is so important.

This righteousness is given through faith in Jesus Christ to all who believe. There is no difference between Jew and Gentile, for all have sinned and fall short of the glory of God, and all are justified freely by his grace through the redemption that came by Christ Jesus.

(Romans 3:22–24)

THE HOME FRONT

JUDGING MIKE

There are many times in life that will remind you that you aren't alone in your fight. It won't always be blaringly in-your-face clear, but you will find that you can't do things on your own all of the time, and usually these reminders are right there in your everyday world.

My cellphone rang at 8:30 a.m. on a Monday morning as I was sipping on a steaming fresh mug of dark roast coffee at the local Panera Bread. The man on the other end of the phone (we'll call him Mike) was audibly upset and wanted to set up a coaching appointment with me, ASAP. I could hear the fear and worry in his voice and so I made a hole in my schedule for later that day.

When the man walked into the office, he looked lost and scared. As I shut the door, he took the chair across the long table from me and began to tell me his situation before I could even ask any questions. He'd been kicked out of his house after his wife discovered he'd been having affairs with a couple of massage therapists who weren't really massage therapists. His wife said that the only way she'd let him back in the house was if he met her conditions:

1. He had to confess his sins to their priest.

2. He had to apologize to their two daughters, her parents, and their friends.

3. He had to agree to meet with a life coach or Christian counselor.

That's how Mike ended up in my office. He needed help and he wanted to be back in his home.

My job as a coach is to listen well, disarm, extend empathy, and ask questions that will hopefully move people toward self-discovery and healthy choices that lead to true, lasting transformation. No matter who I meet with, the unhealthy choices are often the result of two things: coveting (wanting what we don't have) and not understanding our true identity (who we really are). Mike believed that if other women wanted him, he'd have more worth and value and that would somehow make him more of a man—at least that's what he'd heard in locker rooms growing up.

My first question was, "Mike, do you think there can be any sin in heaven?"

He responded quickly, saying, "No."

I stated that God must be pretty righteous (without sin) if there can be no sin in heaven. He agreed. "So Mike," I asked, "how righteous must God be on a scale of one to ten, if ten is the most righteous?"

Again, Mike's answer came quickly: "He'd be a ten."

"Mike, if God is a ten and there can be no sin in heaven, how righteous are you?"

Mike's next response held the key to what he truly believed. He looked up, raised his eyebrows, and said, "Well, after what I've done, I'm probably only a two."

Understanding now that Mike was believing in a works-based theology (good deeds give you more worth and value and bad deeds decrease that value), I asked, "So, if God is a ten and there can be no sin in heaven, how are you going to get to heaven?"

Mike's response was exactly what so many I've worked with have believed, causing them to stay on the hamster wheel of performance in a hopeless attempt to become "good enough."

With a tone that sounded more like a question than an answer, Mike said, "By trying harder?"

The problem with that thinking is that even if you could increase your worth and value in God's eyes by being a better person (having less sin), the highest you could ever achieve on your own would be a 9.9, which still leaves you short of being the required 10 to enter into the kingdom of heaven.

After sharing that with Mike, he looked at me and asked, "Why has no one ever shared that with me before?"

Good question.

The problem with religion or "works-based theology" is that it's made to control us in order to motivate us into a living relationship with Christ. It instills anxiety, shame, guilt, worry, and doubt into the person, creating a fear-based relationship with the Father. And as I said before, you can never truly love someone you're deathly afraid of.

At this point, I went up to the large whiteboard on the wall, grabbed several washable markers, and drew a circle with two more inner circles that resembled an archery target. In the outer ring, I wrote the word *Body*. In the next inner ring, I wrote the word *Soul*. In the center ring, I wrote the word *Spirit*.

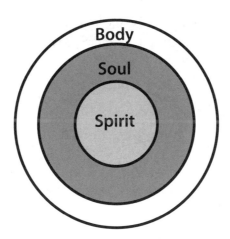

"Mike, First Thessalonians 5:23 tells us that we are made up of three parts: a body (the flesh that we can see), a soul (our mind, where our thoughts, will, and emotions are formed), and our spirit. So Mike, if we know that within our flesh and our mind we have destructive thoughts, unhealthy emotions, and sinful actions, then what part of us would go to heaven?

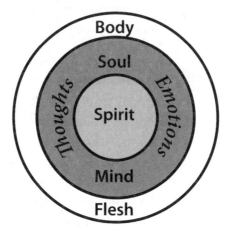

Mike responded, "That would have to be our spirit I'm assuming."

The next question hit the mark. "So, if by your own words, the most you could ever achieve by your good deeds on the 10-point scale is a 9.9, how are you going to be good enough to make it into heaven?"

With the lights going on in Mike's head, he looked up and said, "God would have to do something pretty amazing to make me a 10, but why would He do that after all I've done?"

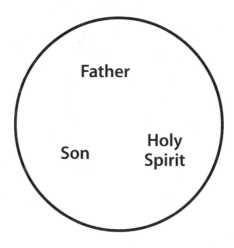

I then drew another circle to the right of the 3-ringed circle and wrote the words *Father, Son,* and *Holy Spirit* inside the circle.

"Mike, God understood there was no way that you could be good enough (righteous) on your own to make it to heaven, no price tag sufficient to cover the cost, and no sacrifice worthy enough for the righteousness of a perfect God. What we deserve as sinners is death. God understood this, but His love for us was so rich and so deep that He decided to send his only Son to take our place, the only sacrifice that would be worthy and just to cleanse us of all our sins."

Jesus took all of mankind's sin upon Himself and was put to death, along with all of our sins that were crucified with Him when He died on the cross. After Jesus was resurrected, God sent His Holy Spirit to inhabit those who would put their faith and trust in Him. He did this to give you His righteousness, to make you into a 10! God came *to you* and *into you* by sending His own Spirit, the Holy Spirit, as a free gift to take the place of your old, sinful spirit. God destroyed the power of sin and death by building a bridge through His Son so that you could be reconciled to Him!

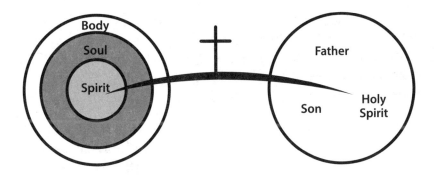

Your true being, your spirit, is now inhabited by God's Spirit, and you have been made totally righteous, completely forgiven, deeply loved, and 100 percent complete in Him. You have everything you will ever need because God is now in you! That is where your "good enough" comes from!

God made him who had no sin to be sin for us, so that in him we might become the righteousness of God.   (2 Corinthians 5:21)

After explaining where our "good enough" comes from, I told Mike a joke that helped him see the foolishness of trying to get our righteousness from our own efforts.

"This guy dies and goes to heaven, and when he arrives, St. Peter is standing at the Pearly Gates. Worried, the man asks St. Peter how many 'points' he has to have in order to get into heaven. St. Peter looks at him, smiles, and says, 'How many points have you got?' The man, now worried and panicked, begins to spout off a list of his good deeds. 'I used to deliver Meals on Wheels to the elderly!' St. Peter smiles, and replies, 'I guess I could give you a point for that.' The man, still panicked, replies, 'What? One point! Ok, uh, I used to volunteer with the Boy Scouts and was an usher on Sunday mornings at church.' St. Peter smiles again, and says, 'I guess I could give you a point for that.' The man is now sweating profusely and listing every good thing he can think of. 'I taught Sunday school; I tithed 15 percent! I even volunteered for nursery duty every month and actually changed poopy diapers!' About that time, another guy who had died walks past the two of them and right through the Pearly Gates and straight into heaven. The man, still listing his good works, becomes livid, turns to St. Peter, and says, 'How many points did that man have?' St. Peter says, 'I don't know. He's not playing this game!'

God made the decision to lay down His own life, to take the bullet for us even when we didn't deserve it. That "gift" is given to us through faith "in Him," not through our own abilities and list of "good works."

For it is by grace you have been saved, through faith—and this is not from yourselves, it is the gift of God—not by works, so that no one can boast. (Ephesians 2:8–9)

Therefore, there is now no condemnation for those who are in Christ Jesus, because through Christ Jesus the law of the Spirit who gives life has set you free from the law of sin and death. For what the law was powerless to do because it was weakened by the flesh, God did by sending his own Son in the likeness of sinful flesh to be a sin offering. And so he condemned sin in the flesh, in order that the righteous requirement

of the law might be fully met in us, who do not live according to the flesh
but according to the Spirit.   (Romans 8:1–4)

Some of those reading this right now might be feeling like Mike should have had more bad consequences in his life, but the consequence of a perfect man, the Son of God, being crucified on your behalf is a big enough consequence, don't you think? And it's possible Mike's wife might have left him, others will despise him, some will gossip, and almost all will judge… but that's their issue. The truth is that Mike was released from the power of sin and death. When Mike finally understood that his sin nature had been replaced with God in him because of that sacrifice, and that his value came from God in him, he realized that he did not need to find that value from other women. As soon as he had that truth to empower him, he no longer needed to look for it elsewhere. In other words, God's grace empowered Mike to move toward obedience!

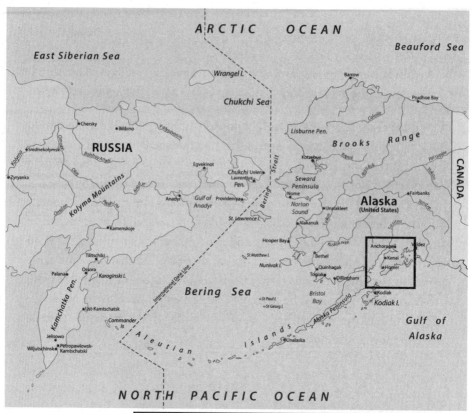

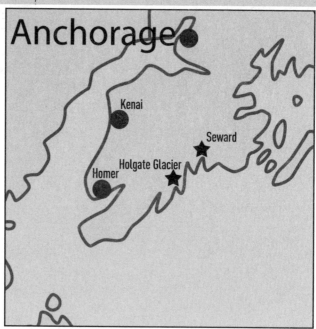

Seward, Alaska and Holgate Glacier

THE WILDS

THINK OR THWIM

I t often seems that when you are the most terrified, the devil has the most lies to tell you. Whether you are fearful of death, losing love in your life, losing your job, or facing a lion or a snake in the wilderness, Satan loves to creep up to you and whisper in your ear all the terrible things that are going to happen to you because you are worthless, not good enough, or a terrible, awful, dirty sinner. It is in those moments that you need to learn to identify his lies and decide whether or not you are going to think or "thwim." When it comes down to it, it's really up to you.

We'd been in Alaska, clamming across from Mt. Redoubt for two days before packing up our gear and heading several hours to the city of Seward, where we were going to go halibut fishing in Resurrection Bay for two days on a 28-foot Bayliner cabin cruiser owned by my friend Ralph. The cruiser was fittingly called the *Think or Thwim*, the same name as his father's commercial fishing boat I worked on out of Bristol Bay, Alaska, in 1985. The shores along Resurrection Bay are even more breathtaking than the shores along Cook Inlet. If you've ever seen the movie *The Hunt for Red October* with Sean Connery, you've seen parts of the bay whether you knew it or not. Its jagged cliffs, seabirds, marine wildlife, and alpine glaciers—especially Bear Glacier—are magnificent.

After a stop at Seward's Three Bears Grocery for a few supplies, we were ready. We lifted a 14-foot Zodiac (a raft Navy SEALS use) onto the bow of the ship, backed her down the launch, set a course for the open ocean, and headed out of the harbor.

Fifteen minutes into the trip, a pod of killer whales appeared off our starboard bow. When a six-foot dorsal fin pops up beside you in three hundred feet of water, it's pretty spooky. Killer whales typically eat sea lions, fish, squid, seals, penguins, dolphins, porpoises, and large whales like the blue whale. They can grow to be thirty feet long, weigh twenty thousand pounds, and swim at speeds of up to thirty miles per hour.

We'd just reached the open ocean, where you could draw a direct line to Japan, when the engine suddenly died. We'd thrown a bearing in the inboard motor and were dead in the water forty miles out from Seward. We had a 25-horsepower Evinrude motor we'd brought along for the Zodiac, but it was a short shaft. It wouldn't work on this bigger boat. The only other motor we had was a 9.9-horsepower trolling motor. We fastened the 9.9 onto the ship's aft and began making a plan.

The skies were growing ominously dark and the troughs of the waves were growing deeper. We knew we needed to find shelter fast. We looked at our GPS and noticed a cove called Three Hole Bay some four miles away that could give us a safe harbor until we could arrange to be rescued.

By the time we made it into the harbor, the mist and fog were as thick as pea soup. The only way we'd have located a rescue boat would have been to run into it. Ship captains and bush pilots will tell you that the weather in Alaska can change quickly and brutally. If you don't have an escape plan, you're toast.

Not only was the main motor kaput, but now we were thirty-five miles out of cellphone range and had no radio contact. We dropped anchor in Three Hole Bay, and spent the night sorting through possible scenarios.

When we awoke the next morning, the boat was only thirty yards from the rocks. Our anchor had come loose. This wasn't an aluminum-hulled boat as most Alaskan boats are. She was made of fiberglass. Hitting those rocks would have been like smacking an egg with a pair of vice grips, a sure recipe for disaster. It was time to "think or thwim."

We used the 9.9 to motor a couple of hundred yards away from the rock cliffs, but now the water was so deep our anchor wouldn't reach bottom. The only option we had was to drop anchor in an avalanche chute, where a massive rock slide had happened years before, piling thousands of boulders to the ocean floor. This could also be a great place to drop a fishing line in case we needed food, as underwater structures tend to hold fish. As my eyes scanned the path of the massive rockslide, all I could think about was the 1958 landslide in Lituya Bay, Alaska, which caused a tsunami higher than the Empire State Building.

The enemy likes to use past events to mess with our minds. He also likes to bring up images of future calamity to cause us unhealthy emotions. Thoughts like: *What if no one finds us here? A landslide has happened here before. What if it happens again while we're anchored in its path? What if our boat drifts into the rocks tonight? What if we run out of fresh water? What if…?* These past and future thoughts can rob you of being present in the moment and cause you to make unhealthy choices based on fear, worry, and doubt.

Three days later, we were able to wave down another boat that was exploring the bay. After sharing our predicament with them, Ralph and his cousin boarded the other boat for a ride back to Seward, leaving just three of us on the *Think or Thwim*. We were sure someone would be back later that night.

It would be two more days before we saw another boat.

On the morning of day five, a fishing boat out of Miller's Landing pulled alongside us and informed us they'd be coming back in twenty-four hours to tow us in. We looked at each other and said, "Hey, we've got twenty-four hours; let's take the Zodiac twelve miles across Aialik Bay to Holgate Glacier." It sounded like a good idea as the skies were clear and we had enough gas for the trip. The three of us grabbed our fishing poles, camera gear, and some snacks and set out across the twelve-mile stretch of ocean.

The journey over there was fairly smooth and we were able to get the Zodiac up on step (riding smoothly in the water) for most of the trip. Some forty-five minutes later, we were approaching Holgate Glacier in the Kenai Fjords. The steep mountains along the fjord were alive with the toes of ancient glaciers snaking down through valleys of cut, grey stone. Waterfalls flowed from beneath their blue tips and careened into the blue-green ocean below. Birds nested on these steep rock faces and their singing echoed throughout the rock cliffs.

As we rounded a curve in the fjord, a massive ice flow began drifting beside our inflatable boat. There in front of us, climbing over five hundred feet skyward, was the face of Holgate Glacier. We were still over a mile away, but it was almost as if you could reach out and touch it.

Within a half-mile of the glacier, we shut off the motor and paddled our way through ice chunks, some as big as pickup trucks and La-Z-Boy recliners, and made our way to a rocky island about a quarter-mile from the face. We decided this would be a safe location to film the face of the glacier.

There were no trees to tie up on, only loose rock to loop our rope around. It never occurred to us that placing the anchor in between two boulders would have been a better choice. Live and learn.

The journey to the top of the rock island took several minutes, as we had to find secure footing, climb ledges, lift gear, and look for a killer spot to set up a camera. Once on top, the view was as good as anything I've ever witnessed.

My friend Wade is great in front of the camera. He's filmed all over the world in some of the deadliest places, and his son, Reed, had an eye for capturing the best nature has to offer.

Wade was standing with his back facing the glacier while being filmed by Reed. I was sitting about twenty yards away, thinking about what I'd say on camera when it came my turn. Wade was on camera describing some crazy story he'd experienced years before when dealing with a glacier. As he was talking, I felt this wave of urgency wash over me: *Go check your boat.*

What? I thought to myself. *Where did that come from?*

Several minutes later, I felt this urgency wash over me once again and a voice said, *Go check your boat.*

Okay, being alone, cold, and stranded is really causing my fear is to mess with me, I thought to myself. Somehow, something about this felt different. Without saying a word, I stood up and began making my way across the top of the rock face. I was just starting to climb down a crevasse using finger holds we'd used on the way up when it happened. Immediately, I knew this was not good.

As I had made my way out of sight of Wade and Reed, a wall of the calving glacier sheared off, and a chunk the size of Walmart thundered into the ocean, creating a wave over twenty feet high. I knew what the sound was instantly and began picking up the pace. When I got within ten yards of the Zodiac, the huge wave hit. It lifted the inflatable so high that the propeller was sticking out of the water. Water surged toward me, almost reaching my feet. As it receded, the rope that had been tied around a rock was now snaking down into the icy water away from the island. If I didn't get to that rope, the raft would float away and end up on some Japanese beach six months from now…and no one knew we were on this barren rock island.

I jumped into the water and plunged my arms down to where I thought the rope must be. As the last foot of rope trailed against the back of my hand, I feverishly grabbed the end of it and began stumbling backward, tripping over partially submerged rocks until my backside struck dry land. I had made a foolish mistake: looping the rope around the rock and thinking it would hold. If I had not listened to that voice that was telling me to go check on the boat, that would have been a second deadly mistake that could have cost me and my friends our lives.

That was our cue; it was time to leave. We'd had enough adventure for one day. The skies were clouding up once again, and we knew we had to make our way back across the bay before things went any further south.

By the time we came out of the mouth of the fjord, the swells were three feet high. In case you don't know, that's too high to get a raft up on step. It had taken us forty minutes to get here, but it was going to take hours to get back to our disabled ship.

The rain was beating against our faces so hard it felt like BB pellets striking our cheeks and hands. Our hoods were pulled as tight around our faces as we could make them, and the mountains across the bay were no longer visible. We were lost. Is that toast I smell?

The good news about being stuck on our boat for the previous five days is that we got a good look at all the cliffs and inlets surrounding Three Hole Bay. Once we got within sight of land, we noticed a rock formation that looked like the keyhole we'd all commented on the day before. That keyhole was a map leading us back to the stranded boat.

When we got to where the boat should have been, it wasn't there. Frantically, we scanned the waters and land structures to try to get our bearings. "There!" Reed pointed. The boat had drifted off the landslide of boulders we'd anchored in and was headed towards the cliffs once again. We had gotten ourselves into all the trouble we could find, and it still wasn't over!

As if we were making the raid on Bin Laden's compound, we quickly pulled up alongside the *Think or Thwim*, and two of us jumped aboard while Wade stayed in the raft. I jumped below deck frantically digging around for extra anchor rope. We'd drifted into much deeper water and the current rope was far too short.

I found another one hundred feet of rope that we could attach to the Zodiac anchor, then drop it over the side of the drifting *Think or Thwim*. I made my way to the bow and began feeding the rope to Wade. In order to securely set an anchor, you have to have the "angle of the dangle" correct. We tried securing the anchor but it wouldn't grab. We were still headed toward the rocks.

"Brent, pull up the second anchor and pass it to me," Wade shouted through the pouring rain. "You tie up your end to the boat. I'm going to motor out with the anchor and drop it about seventy-five yards out so as it sinks it will hopefully catch and hold with the right angle."

Wade disappeared into the heavy fog and pounding rain. I could barely hear his voice but I could still hear the faint sound of the gas motor idling backwards. Within feet of where he was going to drop the anchor over the side, I heard him put the motor in reverse, followed by a loud, "ping." The pin in the motor that allowed it to go into forward and reverse had snapped off.

"Don't drop anchor," I shouted through the rain. "I'll pull you back in." Had that pin sheared off coming back across Aialik Bay during that storm, we'd have been in deep stuff. Had he gone ahead and dropped anchor after the pin broke, he would have drifted out to sea wishing he'd brushed up on his Japanese.

We had one anchor.

That was one of the longest nights of my life. Would we hit the rocks? If we did, could we survive? There was nothing but cliffs surrounding us.

"What if's" filled my mind. That was one of the scariest nights in the wild I'd ever experienced.

That night, we had one anchor. The storm that looked like it was going to smash us against the rocks is what caused our anchor to hit bottom, where it could finally find a secure place.

The anchor held.

Boat in the middle is the intrepid Think or Thwim.

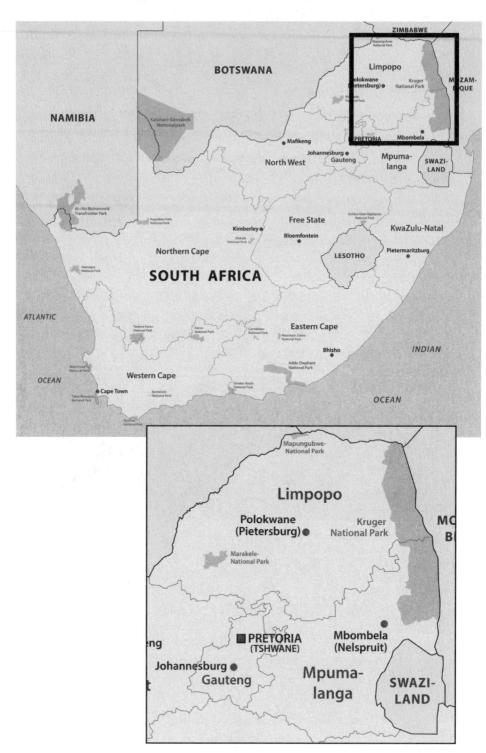

Kruger National Park and Limpopo Province

3

THE BIG LIE

Therefore, there is now no condemnation for those who are in Christ Jesus, because through Christ Jesus the law of the Spirit who gives life has set you free from the law of sin and death.   (Romans 8:1–2)

Knowing God loves us, not because of our good works (performance) but because He created us to be in relationship with Him, demolishes Satan's toxic view he wants us to have of our heavenly Father. When a believer understands he's created in the image of God, deeply loved, totally forgiven, and no longer condemned to death, he is now free of the stifling opinions of others. Free to fail, free to love and be loved without condition. Knowing we are 100 percent complete in Christ is the anti-venom that crushes Satan's biggest lie.

I have a friend who affectionately calls me Brent "Indiana" Henderson. I'd like to think it's because my passion for adventure is like the action hero Indiana Jones, but it's probably related to the fact that I currently live in Indiana, which I affectionately call "the Land of No Adventure."

The Jones who does go by "Indiana" had a memorable line: "Snakes! Why'd it have to be snakes?" If you've seen the adventure classic *Raiders of the Lost Ark*, you probably remember that line. Indiana Jones had a real dislike for those belly-crawlers.

When I was a kid, I used to catch snakes with my hands. Growing up in Pennsylvania, garter snakes and black snakes weren't difficult to find, especially around rock piles and old barns. There are poisonous snakes in Pennsylvania, but rarely are they seen. Because poisonous snakes were so uncommon around my boyhood stomping grounds, I grew up without a fear of snakes. Later in my adulthood, that lack of respect would almost be my undoing.

SNAKES ON A PLAIN

In the early summer 2006, a friend and I had journeyed to South Africa. We were there on safari but most of our time was spent roaming around Kruger National Park. Kruger is about the size of Pennsylvania and home to the deadliest creatures on the planet. If you're looking for serious, heart-pounding adventure, Kruger fills the bill. It's known for its raw beauty, and for being home to the "Big Five."

In Africa, the term "Big Five" was coined by big-game hunters and refers to the five most difficult animals in Africa to hunt on foot: the lion, African elephant, Cape buffalo, leopard, and rhinoceros (white and black). The members of the Big Five were chosen for the difficulty in hunting them and the degree of danger involved, rather than for their size.

The difference between being in the wilds in US lower forty-eight or the long grass of Africa is that is that everything in Africa either wants to stick you or kill you, and it's known for being home to some of the deadliest snakes in the world. The black mamba, boomslang, puff adder, Gaboon viper, and Egyptian cobra are on that list, but the black mamba is definitely the most feared, and for one simple reason: if a black mamba encounters prey or is threatened, it can strike up to twelve times, each time delivering enough neuro- and cardio-toxic venom to kill a dozen men within one hour. Without anti-venom, the mortality rate is 100 percent.

Mambas are incredibly aggressive when cornered and will not hesitate to strike. They can lift two-thirds of their body off the ground and you can't outrun them. It's the largest venomous snake in Africa, with adults reaching an average of eight feet in length. Black mambas aren't actually black but get their name because their mouths are inky black, which they show when threatened. Coming into close contact with a black mamba on this trip was not on my top-100 to-do list.

Before arriving at Dries Visser Safaris, we spent the first week traipsing around Kruger in search of the Big Five. Driving from camp to camp, we were either sleeping in thatched-roof huts or in a seven-foot-square, three-man pole tent. The nighttime sky in the southern hemisphere is breathtaking and takes some getting used to, as the Big Dipper isn't there to guide you. Being south of the equator, it's the constellation known as Crux, or the Southern Cross. There's nothing as invigorating and intimidating as lying beneath the nighttime stars, and hearing the sounds of roaring lions, laughing hyenas, jackals, baboons, and elephants, because it makes you realize that in Africa's darkness, you're at the bottom of the food chain.

After a week of filming and adventuring on the African plains, we headed for Dries Visser Safaris. Their operations are based in the Limpopo Province of South Africa, and about forty minutes north of the town of Thabazimbi. Once we arrived, we were shown our accommodations and promptly met by one of the most fearless animals of South Africa; a Jack Russell Terrier. Jack Russells weigh about fifteen pounds, stand ten to twelve inches high, are longer than they are tall, and they don't have an "off" switch. This little guy would greet me every morning when I stepped outside by dropping a large rock as big as his head at my feet. His favorite game was "fetch the boulder"!

Jack Russells are amazing trackers, and are used to track wounded game on the property. The owner of the safari tells a story from his childhood about a group of their Jack Russells coming into contact with a mamba. Being fearless, the terriers wouldn't back down…and neither would the mamba. The mamba struck every dog, and they all died before they could get them back to the compound. You've really got to pay attention here. Like I said, everything in Africa wants to stick you or kill you.

During the first two days, I was fortunate to harvest the animals I was bowhunting, including a beautiful stallion zebra. Bowhunting at most African safaris is done from elevated blinds and ground or pit blinds. This enables the hunter to make effective shots from cover undetected. The blinds are spacious and dark on the inside, and are situated fifteen to twenty yards from water holes, mineral stations, and game trails. This ensures the hunter of luring in unsuspecting game by catching them in vulnerable positions.

Posing on safari with my zebra.

After harvesting the stallion zebra, we headed back to the compound for the evening meal and stories. Evening meals consisted of real bush cuisine featuring lots of high-protein game meat. Campfires and barbeques happened on a regular basis, and the exotic, nocturnal sounds of the African bush brought home the true African experience.

The evening meal was about to be served when the last safari vehicle pulled in from the day's hunt. It was a father and son from California who'd been on a lion hunt several days before. This particular day, they had been bowhunting a ground blind about a mile away from where I harvested the zebra. As they climbed down from the perch atop the safari truck, I could hear the animation in their voices, and knew something more than the taking of an animal had occurred. I had a feeling this was going to be one of those stories you don't forget.

The father and son team sat down at the table across from us and shortly thereafter, their PH (professional hunter) came over to check on them. It seems that they'd had the rare opportunity to have one of Africa's deadly belly-crawlers grace their blind that day...inside their blind!

As the hot African sun illuminates and warms the plains, night-dwellers and small rodents scurry to find cover, many of them finding shelter in holes dug out by aardvarks or warthogs. The holes are dark, cool, and give the illusion that they provide cover from other predators, especially snakes. Snakes know their prey, and they know these dark holes are the first places they will try to hide. The problem with ground blinds is that they have four solid walls with shooting holes or windows on three sides. Each shooting hole or window is covered with a pantyhose-like material that broadhead arrows can easily penetrate. Each window covering usually has multiple holes where previous hunters have let an arrow fly.

By late morning, the blind had warmed up and the weary bowhunters tipped their chairs back for a short catnap while their PH kept his eyes open for any game on their hit list. It's hard to sit for hours and sometimes days waiting patiently for game without getting sleepy and nodding off. Being inside of one of these stone or cement ground blinds can give you a false sense of security, just as aardvark holes do for rodents. Evidently, these arrow holes leading through the darkened ground blind windows and into the blind were just too much for a passing puff adder to pass up.

With the two hunters sleeping and the PH looking out an opposite window, the adder slithered up the covered window and began snaking its way through one of the arrow holes.

What took place next is something that could give you nightmares. From their sound sleep, the father and son were awaked by a bloodcurdling scream. As the two men opened their eyes, their peripheral vision caught the viper's movement to their right side at about eye level. Without missing a beat, the men were on their feet, dancing around the blind, trying to distance themselves from this camouflaged killer.

The puff adder (*Bitis arietans*) is considered to be Africa's deadliest snake. It is responsible for the most human fatalities, not because they are more venomous than mambas, but because their camouflage is so well-created for their environment that they are the most stepped-on snake in Africa. Puff adders are the Popeye of the snake world, reaching an average length of about only one meter, but with the wide girth and muscular build of Popeye's forearms.

With the two men scurrying around the blind like two cornered mice dropped into a snake-filled aquarium, the PH sprang into action. Almost like he'd done this before, he quickly yanked the fixed broadhead-tipped arrow off the father's bow and plunged it into the viper. As he pulled back on the arrow, he encountered another problem—the arrow had passed through the viper and was now securely lodged in its muscular, jerking body. Luckily, this was a short snake, and the PH was able to pin him down and crush his head. Had this been a mamba, things might have turned out differently as mambas are much longer and more aggressive.

The following evening, Dries Visser Jr. had a special surprise for us. He'd set us up for predator hunt from a fire tower that could be used to hunt jackals and hyenas from a relatively safe, elevated position. However, we'd start hunting for warthogs in the late afternoon from a ground blind, then move to the tower an hour before dark.

Things were slow going in the afternoon. After an hour or so of twiddling our thumbs, my buddy pulled out what he called his secret weapon—a mouse squeaker. After hearing the campfire story the night before about "Popeye the Puff Adder," I really didn't want to take a chance on putting ourselves in the same predicament. Whenever things got slow or I'd start to doze off, he'd depress the mouse squeaker just to get me going.

By 4:00 p.m., we'd had all the fun we could take. The animals had stopped coming to the waterhole, and a shift change was about to take place in the animal kingdom. Darkness was rapidly approaching, so we began packing up our backpacks and preparing to climb up the tower for the twilight predator hunt.

While my friend was setting up a speaker system to play animals in distress calls in a downed tree, I was gathering up our bows and backpacks, and making the climb into the 25-foot-high tower. Climbing was slow going. Because of the gear I was carrying, I only had one free hand to climb with. When I arrived at the top of the ladder, I noticed that the door accessing the tower was only a half-door, as the tower was open all the way around for viewing the property, or, in our case, for hunting.

As I swung the half-door open, a sudden explosion of activity erupted, with feathers and talons flailing. A full-grown African barn owl burst through the opening, leaving me swinging by one hand, desperately grasping for anything to grab onto, and within inches of losing the right side of my face to the owl's talons. As I righted myself, I could see there were at least a half a dozen young owlets, including another adult bird I assumed was the female.

With my attention focused on the young birds, I failed to notice the male bird of prey had circled the tower and abruptly landed on the half-door only two feet from my face. The large bird hurled itself toward me with 43-inch wingspread, almost snapping across my nose as down feathers littered the air like snowflakes. He then proceeded to lean toward my face, head swaying back and forth, hissing and performing bill snaps with eyes nearly squinted shut. After that, I really don't know what happened, but my feet were on the ground before you could count to one.

Needless to say, the evening hunt from this location wasn't going to happen. We packed up our stuff, and arrived back at camp just in time to catch Dries Visser Jr. and tell him our story. Instead of the expected laughter, his face changed into one of relief and he blurted out, "Oh, I'm so glad you're okay. I totally forgot about the owls. Last week, I climbed the tower to check on them, and when I opened the door, a black mamba raised up, and I about fell backward to the ground. I *hate* mambas!"

I don't want to make it seem like there are snakes around every corner and under every rock in Africa—obviously that's not the case or there wouldn't be anyone left alive—but they are there and you'd better be paying attention.

After breakfast, we loaded up the truck and headed some thirty miles toward town. It was good to be in a truck for a while and not in the bush. I relaxed my grip on the steering wheel and settled in for the forty-minute drive, but like I said earlier, everything in Africa wants to stick you or kill you. I'd no sooner relaxed when a curved, moving stick on the road in front of me began to rise up off the ground. *You've got to be kidding me*, I thought. *What are the odds of another mamba crossing our path?*

We'd no sooner passed the mamba when my buddy said, "Brent, stop the truck. Let's see if we can catch him!" Okay, I may not be the sharpest tool in the shed, but I recognized this was a bad idea. Before I knew what was happening, my friend was yelling for me to get out the video camera. By the time I removed the lens cap, he'd already pinned the viper's head to the ground with a forked-stick, and had slid his hand down to shut the lid on this coffin-mouthed killer.

Within seconds of hitting record, the nine-foot-long mamba wrapped itself around his arm. It was like a moment from *Wild Kingdom*, an adventure TV show I watched as a kid. The host was Marlin Perkins, and with his sidekick, Jim Fowler, by his side, Marlin would say something like, "I'll stay here in the truck while Jim wrestles the giant anaconda!" Well, in this instance, my friend played the role of Jim while I kept my distance and ran the camera.

Several minutes of monologue passed when a local pickup truck drove up. My friend thought it would be a good idea to have a little fun with these guys, and when they pulled up beside him, he held the snake toward their window, saying, "Hey, look at this really neat black snake I found!"

When these locals saw the mamba wrapped around his arm, they began shouting things like, "You stupid American!" and "That's a *blankety-blank* mamba, you fool! Please kill it when you're done messing around" as mamba's kill many Africans every year. With a few more "blan-kety-blanks," the driver put the truck in gear and hit the gas.

This was a "Kodak moment." Why should my friend get all the glory shots? I pulled out my camera, took the mamba from him, and had my own hero shots taken. After all, this was a crazy story and impressive photo opportunity I could use for speaking events! After posing with this killer, and after seeing the fear in people's eyes and the dread in their voices, I pulled out my hunting knife and drove the tip down through the viper's head, accented with a little twist at the end. After filming one more clip with my friend holding the mamba, he tossed him into the long grass and we were on our way.

A few minutes down the road, I noticed something running down the back of my hand. Upon further inspection, I realized I was looking at a mix of blood and venom. The first thought that went through my mind was, *Hmm, I wonder. If I have an open cut on my hand, can I be envenomed with these deadly toxins?* As soon as I vocalized my concerns, my friend was inspecting his hand as well, as he'd had an open wound on his hand from several days before. Before another thought crossed my mind, I slammed on the brakes, and we both jumped out of the vehicle and began feverously dousing our hands with Coca-Cola before the venom-ous cocktail could trickle into our open wounds. Coke—"Always the real thing!"

Holding a live, deadly black mamba in 2006. Dumbest things I've ever done.

Let me remind you, black mamba venom is extremely potent and can kill a full-grown adult in less than half-an-hour. Since most snake bites happen in remote areas where the nearest hospital is at least an hour's drive away, the mortality rate of mamba bites is high. Nearly 100 percent of victims die.

How foolish were we? What drove my friend to do something as crazy as to hand-catch one of the deadliest snakes in the world? Why did I film it? Why did I have to have my hero shot taken with the belly-crawler as well?

When you think about the snake we were toying with, it really was absolute stupidity. We both knew the dangers involved, and we both could have been hammered by the deadly viper in a split second, and neither of us had anti-venom or knew where to find it.

Months after the encounter, the two of us discussed why in the world we would take such a crazy risk. One of the reasons we landed on was that both of us had grown up watching *Wild Kingdom* and having others think we were just as courageous as Jim Fowler would somehow bring us a sense of higher worth and value than just being like Marlin Perkins sitting in the truck.

And then there's the issue of me getting my picture taken with the deadly belly-crawler. Why did I have to have a hero shot? Probably for the same reason we took the risk in the first place—fame and glory. It's the same driving reason why so many people do crazy things while their friends film them, and then post it on the Internet in hopes that it goes viral. And, just like on the TV show *Cheers*, we want to be where "everybody knows your name." We want to be famous.

As deadly as the venomous black mamba's strike is, there is another serpent whose strike doesn't leave a visible mark. This serpent's name is Satan, and he is *"the father of lies"* (John 8:44). His mouth is even darker than the mouth of the mamba, and his silent, venomous strike affects 100 percent of all humans, poisoning them with fear, coveting, and shame.

You don't have to look far to find his first victim. It's recorded in the book of Genesis at the very beginning of mankind.

Now the serpent was more crafty than any beast of the field which the LORD God had made. And he said to the woman, "Indeed, has God said, 'You shall not eat from any tree of the garden'?" The woman said to the serpent, "From the fruit of the trees of the garden we may eat; but from the fruit of the tree which is in the middle of the garden, God has

said, 'You shall not eat from it or touch it, or you will die.'" The serpent
said to the woman, "You surely will not die! For God knows that in the
day you eat from it your eyes will be opened, and you will be like God,
knowing good and evil." When the woman saw that the tree was good
for food, and that it was a delight to the eyes, and that the tree was desirable to make one wise, she took from its fruit and ate; and she gave
also to her husband with her, and he ate. Then the eyes of both of them
were opened, and they knew that they were naked; and they sewed fig
leaves together and made themselves loin coverings. They heard the
sound of the LORD God walking in the garden in the cool of the day,
and the man and his wife hid themselves from the presence of the LORD
God among the trees of the garden. Then the LORD God called to the
man, and said to him, "Where are you?" He said, "I heard the sound
of You in the garden, and I was afraid because I was naked; so I hid
myself." And He said, "Who told you that you were naked? Have you
eaten from the tree of which I commanded you not to eat?" The man
said, "The woman whom You gave to be with me, she gave me from the
tree, and I ate." Then the LORD God said to the woman, "What is this
you have done?" And the woman said, "The serpent deceived me, and
I ate."   (Genesis 3:1–13 NASB)

God's command to Adam: "You must not eat from the tree of the
knowledge of good and evil, for when you eat from it you will certainly
die." It didn't take long for the serpent to envenomate Eve with confusion
and lies: "*Indeed, has God said, 'You shall not eat from any tree of the garden?'*"

After Eve reminds the serpent, "*God has said, 'You shall not eat from it
or touch it, or you will die,'*" Satan sinks his fangs in all the way. "*You surely
will not die! For God knows that in the day you eat from it your eyes will be
opened, and you will be like God, knowing good and evil.*"

After rereading this several times, the thing that stood out to me was
when the Lord God called out to the man, asking him, "*Where are you?*"
Adam replied, "*I heard the sound of You in the garden, and I was **afraid** because I was naked; so **I hid myself**.*" The next question is key: "*Who told you
that you were naked?*"

Until this point, Adam and Eve had walked through the garden feeling no shame or fear. In one vicious strike, the enemy's lies left them both hiding in shame and afraid of their Creator.

In John 8:44, Jesus clarifies Satan's true nature:

He was a murderer from the beginning, not holding to the truth, for there is no truth in him. When he lies, he speaks his native language, for he is a liar and the father of lies.

Satan's lies affects all of us, from Adam and Eve to this day, and until the day we go home to be with Jesus. Robert McGee, in his book, *The Search for Significance*, identifies Satan's biggest lie:

My Performance + Others' Opinions = My Self-Worth

If and when we buy into this lie, it causes us deep shame and fear of not being good enough.

The truth is that it's not our performance (what we do) or other's opinions that matter, but *God's performance and God's opinion* that completes us and give us our worth and value. Like I said earlier, when God's Spirit came into my spirit the moment I truly believed, I was made 100 percent righteous *in Him*. This truth was paid for, stamped and sealed in blood. Therefore, I no longer have to try to get man's approval to find my "good enough." Here's the anti-venom to Satan's big lie:

God's Performance + God's Opinion = My Self-Worth

The apostle Paul nails the coffin shut on Satan's "Big Lie" in Galatians 2:

What actually took place is this: I tried keeping rules and working my head off to please God, and it didn't work. So I quit being a "law man" so that I could be God's man. Christ's life showed me how, and enabled me to do it. I identified myself completely with him. Indeed, I have been crucified with Christ. My ego is no longer central. It is no longer important that I appear righteous before you or have your good opinion, and I am no longer driven to impress God. Christ lives in me. The life you see me living is not "mine," but it is lived by faith in the Son of God, who loved me and gave himself for me. I am not going to go back on that. Is it not clear to you that to go back to that old rule-keeping, peer-pleasing religion would be an abandonment of everything personal and free in my relationship with God? I refuse to do that, to repudiate God's grace. If a living relationship with God could come by rule-keeping, then Christ died unnecessarily. (Galatians 2:19–21 MSG)

DISCOVERING WHAT YOU'RE WORTH

Modern thinking and motivational speakers will tell you that in order for a person to have a positive view of self, they must learn to accept themselves, love themselves, and develop self-esteem. That's their solution to a happy life. The problem is that it's nearly impossible for us to "like" ourselves when we think, feel, and act so badly—repeatedly. Author, friend, and mentor, Derek Wilder, in his book, *Freedom*, states, "Convincing ourselves that we are good enough, just the way we are, becomes a futile pursuit. So, we naturally turn to other people's opinions as a gauge for whether we are being 'good enough.'"[5]

Men typically take their self-worth questions to Eve—to women. The problem with that is if you give her, or anyone, that kind of power, one moment they will make you feel like the hero, and the next moment a zero. Take a look at this quote: "If my self-worth has anything to do with what you think of me, 100 percent of the time I will try and manipulate you to get my needs met." This is exactly what happens when we try to get our question answered outside of God.

When we find ourselves attempting to get our self-worth from others, it creates within us unhealthy emotions, like fear, anxiety, depression, worry, and doubt. It's a trap the enemy has set for us, and as long as we keep looking to others for validation of "who we are," there will be no solution. We will constantly be stuck in Satan's hamster wheel of performance, trying to manipulate others to get their good opinions. And we know what snakes do to hamsters.

It's important to remember that our self-worth must align with God's appraisal of us, not with the assessments of our friends, family, spouse, boss, pastor, or anyone else.

---

5. Derek Wilder, *Freedom* (Litchfield, IL: Revival Waves of Glory Books & Publishing, 2009).

God's Spirit touches our Spirit and confirms who we really are. We know who he is, and we know who we are: Father and children.

(Romans 8:16 MSG)

Notice Paul's language: God's *Spirit* touches our spirit and confirms *who* we really are. Not what the world says we are, including social media. Not what our actions indicate, like being the hero in a dangerous situation. We must learn who we really are at our core, our essence, our *spirit*.

The salvation of God creates a total core transformation, and a radical remaking of a person's identity.

Let this salvation statement sink in:

+ I am a new creation of infinite worth.

+ I am completely forgiven.

+ I am fully pleasing to God.

+ I am totally accepted by God. And I am absolutely complete.

+ I am righteous.

+ I am completely loved. There is nothing I can do or say that will make God love me more. There is nothing I can do or say to make God love me less.

+ I am what God says I am. This is God's truth, and God's truth is unchanging, incorruptible, and indestructible. It is the ever-living Word of God.

This radical redefining of ourselves is the missing piece of the astute and well-meaning secular therapists and self-help gurus. It is this new identity through the indwelling of the Holy Spirit that gives us the logic and the strength to believe we are good enough to accept ourselves, to love ourselves, and to develop a healthy self-esteem even in the face of our unhealthy thoughts, feelings, and actions. This is what provides the transformative power to experience true freedom in Christ. This is what breaks us free of the prison walls we build around ourselves. The redeeming power of God's grace is the dangerous truth that transforms our lives.

Guys, let me tell you this. The only opinion that matters is from the One whose opinion doesn't change. In His mind, if you are a believer in Christ, you are perfect and you always will be. Sure, hero shots are great, and I'm probably not going to stop taking them, and neither are you. But remembering that our self-worth doesn't come from our performance, the number of "likes" we get on Facebook, or how many followers we have on Twitter, but instead, our value found "in Christ" creates a healthy core and a secure identity.

So, when the enemy tries to deceive you into believing that your worth and value come from your performance or others' opinions, *"take up the full armor of God that you may be able to resist in the evil day"* (Ephesians 6:13 NASB). Be strong in who you are so that when you are faced with that idiot snake that tries to make you feel like a mouse, you can stand up and roar like the lion you were intended to be.

INTO THE WILDS FIELD GUIDE

CHAPTER THREE: THE BIG LIE

1.   What's the dumbest thing you've ever done to impress others?

2.   What were you hoping to get out of that behavior?

3.   Where do you find yourself still trying to impress others, and why do you think you need to do that?

Here's where the enemy strikes us the most with his deadly venom:

The Big Lie

My Performance + Others' Opinions = My Self-Worth

Here's the antivenin to Satan's poisonous lies:

The Big Truth

God's Performance + God's Opinion = My Self-Worth

In chapter three, we talked about how convincing ourselves that we are good enough just the way we are, and how that becomes a futile pursuit. So, we naturally turn to other people's opinions as a gauge for whether or not we are being "good enough."

4.   To whom or to what do you find yourself typically taking your self-worth questions to get answered? (Women, your job, kids, athletics, money, your body, etc...)

Read Paul's words from Galatians 2:19–31 (MSG):

What actually took place is this: I tried keeping rules and working my head off to please God, and it didn't work. So I quit being a "law man" so that I could be God's man. Christ's life showed me how, and enabled me to do it. I identified myself completely with him. Indeed, I have been crucified with Christ. My ego is no longer central. It is no longer important that I appear righteous before you or have your good opinion, and I am no longer driven to impress God. Christ lives in me. The life you see me living is not "mine," but it is lived by faith in the Son of God, who loved me and gave himself for me. I am not going to go back on that.

Is it not clear to you that to go back to that old rule-keeping, peer-pleasing religion would be an abandonment of everything personal and free in my relationship with God? I refuse to do that, to repudiate God's grace. If a living relationship with God could come by rule-keeping, then Christ died unnecessarily.

5.   Paul states that he tried keeping rules and working his rear off to please God, but it didn't work. Where in your life do you find yourself trying to please God by performing the right actions? (Examples: tithing, church attendance, abstinence from tobacco or alcohol or chew, or going out with girls that do, etc.)

6.   Paul realized that his ego got in the way when he was attempting to "appear righteous," because it was all about himself. Do you find yourself struggling to do good to get others' attention or God's good opinion?

7.   If you truly understood that this life you're living is not really yours but that you belong to God—that Christ "in you" is your true identity, and that God loves you so much that He gave Jesus to die in your place (before you were born and had done anything good or bad)—would you still need to strive to get others' good opinions?

8. Whose is the only opinion that matters? Why?

It's important to remember that our self-worth must align with God's appraisal of us, not with the assessment of our friends, family, spouse, boss, pastor, or anyone else.

God's Spirit touches our spirits and confirms who we really are. We know who he is, and we know who we are: Father and children.

(Romans 8:16 MSG)

Because of Satan's lies, we must renew our minds daily to radically reidentify ourselves "in Christ," and not in our performance. Read the following salvation statements aloud:

+ I am a new creation of infinite worth.

+ I am completely forgiven.

+ I am fully pleasing to God.

+ I am totally accepted by God. I am absolutely complete.

+ I am righteous.

+ I am completely loved. There is nothing I can do or say that can make God love me more. There is nothing I can do or say that can make God love me less.

+ I am who God says I am. This is God's truth, and God's truth is unchanging, incorruptible, and indestructible. It is the ever-living Word of God.

9. How did reading those truths out loud make you feel about your worth and value?

10. If you really believe that "Christ in you" is your true identity, do you need to keep trying to impress others? How radically is that going to change your life, and in what areas?

4

FLAMING ARROWS

In addition to all this, take up the shield of faith, with which you can extinguish all the flaming arrows of the evil one. (Ephesians 6:16)

He was a murderer from the beginning, and does not stand in the truth because there is no truth in him. Whenever he speaks a lie, he speaks from his own nature, for he is a liar and the father of lies.

(John 8:44 NASB)

One of my hunting companions tells a story about tent camping with some friends on Kodiak Island, Alaska, while bowhunting. After everyone crawled into their sleeping bags, he walked around and noticed a guy's head bulging like a melon against the wall of a small nylon tent. He reached his hand out and cupped it over the man's head and said quietly, "Research has shown that when bears attack campers in tents, they always try to identify the head for the first bite." The lump on the wall of the tent suddenly disappeared. Unhealthy thoughts were getting into that man's head.

Have you ever had an unhealthy thought suddenly burst into your mind? Have you ever wondered where the thought came from? Did it come from you or from somewhere else? Did the thought leave you feeling ashamed, condemned, conflicted, or even afraid? It's important that we discover where our unhealthy thoughts come from.

ENTERTAINING LITTLE LIES

Guys like attention. When you are married, and especially if you have kids, you don't always get the attention that you feel like you need from your wife. You know she loves you, but life can get crazy sometimes, and it's not always easy to stay enthusiastic 100 percent of the time. It's at that exact moment, when you are feeling like you aren't getting enough attention, that the enemy will push little lies into your thoughts to send you his own negative message. You are feeling the "poor me's" and suddenly your old high school girlfriend wants to be Facebook friends, and sends a message to you about how she can't believe you are still such a stud. (Okay, so maybe she didn't call you a "stud" specifically, but you and I both know that's what she meant.) This is the opportunity for the enemy to strike. With just a few computer clicks and a "you look great too" response, you could start something that could easily turn into something worse. All so you can get a little bit of your ego stroked. You know it's not worth it, but it sure feels good at the time, doesn't it?

This is how the enemy gets into our head, just like my friend grabbing the man's head from outside the tent. But where are these thoughts coming from?

How many of us have unhealthy thoughts on a daily basis? Most of us do—even believers do. Why? Where are they coming from? They don't have to be unhealthy sexual thoughts. They could be normal thoughts: *If I just had more money, I would have more value,* or *Boy, that third Krispy Kreme doughnut sure would make me feel better right now!*

If you look at things through God's lens, you'll see that all of those unhealthy thoughts are based on coveting—wanting what we don't have. Where are these thoughts coming from? Does it make me a bad person because these thoughts sometimes burst into my head?

Let me ask you a question. If you're a believer in Jesus Christ, do you want to be having those unhealthy thoughts? What about God? Does He want you to have those thoughts? I think the answer in both cases in an emphatic "NO." If we don't want to have them, and we know they aren't coming from God, where are they coming from?

You've got it: Satan.

So, how does the enemy keep us bound to his lies? One way he does it by what we'll call unhealthy "past and future thinking." I want to clarify this issue for you. You can have *healthy* past and future thoughts. For example, remembering the day my son caught his first fish or imagining myself walking my daughter down the aisle at her wedding are healthy and appropriate thoughts. In this application, however, we are focusing on past and future flaming arrows that are lies from Satan.

Here are a few examples of past thoughts that might keep you awake:

+ *If only I'd listened better to my parents when I was young, I might not be in this current position.*

+ *If only I hadn't bought that new car, I probably wouldn't be in this financial bind.*

+ *Maybe if I'd treated my wife differently, she wouldn't have left me and taken the kids.*

+ *What if the bank forecloses on my house?*

+ *What if my spouse leaves me?*

+ *What if my daughter gets pregnant?*

+ *What if my son gets into drugs?*

DEBUGGING YOUR BRAIN

How do we fight back? Mostly, we try to cover up those unhealthy thoughts and emotions by watching TV, looking at porn, overworking, overeating, excessive drinking, or some other unhealthy behavior. If the enemy can keep you busy trying to put out his past and future arrows, he's got you.

It's important that you understand something. You live in the present, and so does God. You don't live in the past or the future, therefore past and future thinking can keep you locked in an emotional prison. Look at what the Bible says in Matthew 6:34 about worrying about tomorrow:

Therefore do not worry about tomorrow, for tomorrow will worry about itself. Each day has enough trouble of its own.

Here's another passage from James 4:13–14:

Come now, you who say, "Today or tomorrow we will go to such and such a city, and spend a year there and engage in business and make a profit." Yet you do not know what your life will be like tomorrow. You

are just a vapor that appears for a little while and then vanishes away.
Instead, you ought to say, "If the Lord wills, we will live and also do this
or that." (NASB)

In C. S. Lewis's book *The Screwtape Letters*, Satan is trying to teach his
demonic nephew how to tempt and destroy Christians. The enemy states,

> Our business is to get them away from the eternal, and from the
> Present. We sometimes tempt a human…to live in the Past. But
> this is of limited value, for they have some real knowledge of the
> past and it has a determinate nature and, to that extent, resembles
> eternity. It is far better to make them live in the Future. Biological
> necessity makes all their passions point in that direction already,
> so that thought about the Future inflames hope and fear. Also, it is
> unknown to them, so that in making them think about it we make
> them think of unrealities. In a word, the Future is, of all things, the
> thing least like eternity. It is the most completely temporal part of
> time—for the Past is frozen and no longer flows, and the Present
> is all lit up with eternal rays.[6]

In essence, he's saying, "If we can just get them to live in fear of the
future, and not in the present, we've got them!" Don't sleep with your
head bulging against the tent wall. Make good decisions. Live in the now.
Otherwise, the enemy grabs us by the head and begins to sink his lies deep
into our thoughts. This is not just simply about "doing the right thing."
When the desire is removed to do the wrong thing, you will do the right
thing!

Nearly all unhealthy emotions are rooted in the future, but many are
rooted in our past. Regret causes us to look to the past, while fear, anxiety,
doubt, worry, and the like cause us to be trapped in future thinking. So,
how do we fight back?

Paul talked about this form of spiritual attack in Ephesians 6:16 when
he wrote, "*In addition to all this, take up the shield of faith, with which you can
extinguish all the flaming arrows of the evil one.*" Those flaming arrows are the

---

6. C. S. Lewis, *The Screwtape Letters* (New York: HarperCollins Publishers, 1942,
restored 1996), 68.

thoughts Satan sends at our minds. Paul didn't make up the arrow story. In ancient times, Roman archers used flaming arrows to intimidate opposing armies. A variety of materials were used to ignite arrows. One method was to pour melted pitch, or tar, on an arrowhead, allow it to harden, and then ignite it before shooting the arrow. Those arrows didn't kill many men, but the effect was exactly as anticipated. Intimidation! Fear can paralyze.

Our military uses fear and intimidation today in the war on terror. There are YouTube videos of the US armed forces flying choppers at night and watching bad guys in hostile territories planting an IED (improvised explosive device.) We can see them setting the bomb and then hear the command to take them out. Next, a silent Apache chopper sprays them with a 30-mm chain gun from a half-mile away. The result is carnage and fear. When the bad guys watch this footage on the Internet, they know that there is an unseen force that is vigilant about stopping them in their tracks.

Our Predator drone strikes are another weapon of intimidation. One day, some bad guys identified by a pilot sitting at a desk at an Air Force base in Nevada via a drone flying at twenty-five thousand feet above the Afghan sand. Seconds later, a Hellfire missile closes in on them. That's a modern-day flaming arrow with the same intended effect. We are getting into their heads and implanting a fear of the unknown future.

Unhealthy thoughts are not new. When I was a kid, I'd sometimes lie awake at night worrying about some bigger kid who threatened to kick my butt at school the next day, just because. Then there was the fear that I would not be accepted by the cool kids and be shoved out of their circle and made fun of because I was not an athlete or extremely skinny. Or that I'd be chosen last again in gym class, as sides were picked for the basketball game. I spent a lot of time worrying about *what ifs*. Satan's barrage of lies is not new.

As I've grown older, the thoughts that keep me awake at night have changed. They've gone from childhood fears to adult nightmares haunted with new worries about the future. Thoughts like *What if I can't make my house payment this month?* or *What if I lose my job tomorrow?* Sometimes our unhealthy thoughts connect to the past and regret: *Why didn't I pursue what I really wanted to do rather than being stuck in this dead end job?* or *If I had married the girl from down the street, would my life be better?* One train of thought is about the future: the *what ifs*. The other is about the past: the *what might have beens*. Both are based on unknowns. Satan's arrows often come from the *what ifs*.

Satan knows how to keep you awake at night and often aims arrows at your mind in an effort to disrupt your life. If he can land a flaming arrow, he knows the blaze can spread like wildfire. One minute we are worrying about one situation, then that worry spreads to another problem, and then another. Sometimes Satan's plan is to just keep us staring at the sky, and worrying about another flaming arrow. Satan is the great deceiver (see Revelation 20:8–10) and the father of lies (see John 8:44). He would love to derail you with fears, doubts, and untrue thoughts. The resulting actions from those feelings can be disastrous unless we learn how to take him out!

INTO THE WILDS FIELD GUIDE

CHAPTER FOUR: FLAMING ARROWS

He was a killer from the very start. He couldn't stand the truth because there wasn't a shred of truth in him. When the Liar speaks, he makes it up out of his lying nature and fills the world with lies.

(John 8:44 MSG)

Jesus makes it clear that Satan is the father of lies, and that when he whispers to us, he fills us with his lies.

1.   Have you ever had an unhealthy thought suddenly "burst" into your head? Where do you think that thought came from?

2.   If Christ is in you, and He is your true identity, did that unhealthy thought come from the real you? Did God cause you to think it? If not, who else?

3.   When you had that unhealthy thought, how did it make you feel? Ashamed, condemned, conflicted, lustful, guilty, afraid, or something else? (Write down the unhealthy emotion created by that thought. It's vital that you identity how that thought made you feel, as we will soon discover).

4.   What we think shapes how we feel and act. What unhealthy actions came out of having the emotion(s) you just identified?

5.   What were the consequences from your unhealthy actions?

In Ephesians 6:16, Paul states, *"In addition to all this, take up the shield of faith, with which you can extinguish all the flaming arrows of the evil one."*

6.   What do you think it means to *"take up the shield of faith"*?

7.   Many men I've spoken with believe taking up the shield of faith means "trying harder." What actions do you take to thwart the arrows/lies of the evil one? (For example, going to church, praying more, confessing your sins, memorizing scripture, getting baptized, casting out the evil one, getting involved in a small group, etc.) How's that working for you?

Those are all good things, but they have very little to do with extinguishing the flaming arrows of the evil one. Romans 12:2 tells us that we are to renew our minds so that we can be transformed.

8.   Whose job is it to do the transforming? Whose job is it to do the renewing?

The enemy's lies are incredibly predictable. He always likes to cause us to keep us thinking about past or future events. I want you to try something for a second. Try to have an unhealthy emotion. The only stipulation: you're not allowed to think about something from your past or the future.

Go!

You weren't able to conjour an unhealthy emotion, were you?

Why? Because God wants us to stay in the present, with Him. He instructs us not to fret about tomorrow (future worries) in Matthew 6:34, and He's assured us that He's forgiven us of our mistakes and sins (past regrets) in 1 John 1:9.

If the enemy can keep you feeling worthless through shame, fear, and condemnation, he can keep you stuck in an unhealthy state. Part of untwisting the lies and renewing our mind is finding the advantages in difficult situations. In the columns below, first write down a difficult situation you're currently going through, then list the disadvantages it's creating. Finally, carefully look at the situation to find the advantages the disadvantage is creating.

Example:

Difficult Situation:

I lost my job

Disadvantages	Advantages
I'm currently unemployed and worried about money.	I finally have time to search for a better job.
I'm worried about my house payment.	This circumstance is teaching me the importance of managing my money.
	My situation is causing me to spend more time talking to God.
	I am learning to trust God more.

Ultimately, the reason we sin is because we're coveting—we're wanting what we don't have. We do this because the enemy doesn't want us to remember that "in Christ," we have everything we'll ever need. If we realized we're 100 percent complete in Christ, it would be game over for Satan.

Renewing our mind with truth causes us to focus on the gift instead of the challenge. Read the following verse:

Since Jesus went through everything you're going through and more, learn to think like him. Think of your sufferings as a weaning from that old sinful habit of always expecting to get your own way. Then you'll be able to live out your days free to pursue what God wants instead of being tyrannized by what you want.   (1 Peter 4:1–2 MSG)

9. If you choose to only focus on the disadvantage, what happens to your emotions? What unhealthy actions might happen as a result of unhealthy thoughts?

10. What happened to your emotions after identifying the advantages found in your difficult situation? What healthy actions might come about as a result of focusing on healthy thoughts?

Finally, brothers and sisters, whatever is true, whatever is noble, whatever is right, whatever is pure, whatever is lovely, whatever is admirable—if anything is excellent or praiseworthy—think about such things. (Philippians 4:8)

The purpose of having an experienced guide is to help you find your way through the wilderness. In the next chapter, we're going to learn how replacing the lies with God's Word enables us to take up the shield of faith to extinguish those flaming arrows before they can land.

THE HOME FRONT

ADVANTAGES AND DISADVANTAGES

I had just finished speaking at a church service in Southern California when a man walked up to me and asked if I could spare a few minutes to speak with a gentleman in an adjacent room who was very distraught. As I walked into the room, the man was on his knees shaking with fear as tears of shame poured down his face. Another man knelt beside him, telling the broken man that the reason his wife left him was because he had become too liberal, and had allowed alcohol and pornography into his home via the Internet. If this man had only repented enough to his family and church, rid his home of anything that was allowing his mind to wander (but wait, there's more), got himself into an accountability group with other men, prayed more; memorized more Scripture, attended a 12-step group, and submitted to weekly counseling...then his wife might let him back in the house. I'm exhausted just thinking about all that stuff!

Now, there is nothing wrong with a lot of what that man was saying. It would be good to weed out negative influences, get some counseling, pray, know God's Word, maybe even attend a recovery group, and get professional help, but the core issue here isn't "trying harder." The issue is: why did the man believe the lies that alcohol and pornography would solve his problems in the first place?

As the two men prayed together, I quietly walked over to the well-meaning friend who was praying in a loud, shaming voice over the man who was crying. I placed my hand on his shoulder. He opened his eyes, and I asked him if I could have a few minutes alone with the distraught man. After he left the room, I gently and quickly locked the door behind him. There didn't need to be any more shame or fear-based religion heaped on this broken man.

I pulled up a chair to this man we'll call Tom. He looked up at me through puffy, bloodshot eyes, and I simply asked him to share what had happened to him. Tom told me that his wife had kicked him out of the house after finding porn on the computer history. He admitted he'd struggled with it in the past, but hadn't looked at it for over ten months until a couple days prior. When his wife found the evidence, she immediately began crying, called her mother, and proceeded to tell Tom that he had to leave the house and couldn't return until he got help for his addiction. Tom also shared with me that he'd been asked to step down from any leadership within the church, including teaching Sunday school and ushering. He was scared and humiliated.

After listening to Tom for a few minutes, I asked if I could have a few more minutes of his time and he nodded his head. Behind Tom in the classroom where we were seated was a large chalkboard. I had Tom spin his chair around and I stood and drew two columns on the board. One was labeled "advantages" and the other "disadvantages." I then asked Tom a question: "What are the disadvantages of your situation right now?" He looked at me with this "Are you serious?" look on his face, and then he proceeded to regurgitate what he'd been telling me.

"Well, my wife kicked me out of our home and said I can't return until I get help for my addiction." So, I wrote that in the disadvantages column.

I asked for more disadvantages. Tom said his wife had paid all the bills and now he was going to have to learn how to do that. He also told me that she did all the grocery shopping, and he'd never done that in the fifteen years they'd been married. After writing down that he was going to have to take responsibility for paying bills and buying groceries, I asked him if there were any other disadvantages. He then shared with me again about the church asking him to step down from his position of leadership.

After writing that one in the disadvantages column, he shrugged his shoulders and said, "I guess that's about it."

I next asked Tom what were the advantages to his circumstances. Tom looked up, shook his head, and replied with a look of shock on his face: "What? Are you serious? Advantages?"

"Tom, your wife said you can't come home until you get help for your addiction. What are you going to do?"

Tom replied, "I've already made an appointment with a counselor to get help."

I asked, "Is it a good thing or a bad thing you're going to get help for your issue?"

"It's a good thing."

"Great Tom, that's an advantage!" I removed that item from his disadvantages column and moved it into his advantages column.

"What about having to take responsibility for paying your bills? Is learning to be responsible a good thing or a bad thing?"

"I guess you're going to tell me it's a good thing," Tom said, smirking.

"Absolutely," I said. "Okay, what about not knowing how to shop for groceries?"

"I know, I know, it's a good thing to learn how to shop for my own groceries," Tom laughed. "But, what about being asked to step down from the church leadership. I'm totally humiliated about that."

I then asked Tom if humility was a good thing or a bad thing.

As his shoulders relaxed, Tom took in a deep breath and stated, "It's a good thing."

With that, I moved the last disadvantage into the advantage column.

Tom looked at the chalkboard and shook his head in disbelief. "How did you do that?" he asked. The look of fear and shame on his face was changing into a look of relief and hope.

"Tom," I said, "God never uses fear and condemnation to change your behavior, because He knows that doing so will drive you deeper into hiding. He knows that the worse you feel about yourself, the more you'll be tempted to run to something unhealthy that will make you feel better for a brief moment, like when you ran to porn. God cares more about you having a relationship with Him than He does about trying to get you to have the right behavior. God doesn't want you to 'fake it till you make it'; He wants you to know Him, and He wants you to know who you really are—your true identity, Christ in you. Whenever others try and label you by your sin, what does that make you feel?"

"Shame and fear, that I'm not good enough," Tom replied.

"And how does it make you feel to know that there is nothing you can do or say that will make God love you less, or love you more?"

"I don't feel afraid anymore! I feel deeply loved and forgiven, like my identity comes from Him and not from my sin! It's amazing to believe that someone could love me that much, or be that kind to me in spite of my failures. That kind of love makes me feel complete, like I don't need a beautiful woman or a church's approval to make me feel that I'm good enough. I wish I'd have had a safe enough place to share my shortcomings and temptations before this all blew up. Isn't that supposed to be the church?"

"Yes, Tom, it is...."

So what was it that flipped the "truth switch" in Tom's thinking that brought him to a place of peace, hopefulness, and repentance?

Was it a man who was judging and shaming him by bringing up his sins, and giving him a to-do list to regain right standing? No.

Was it dwelling on the depth of how sinful he was, the threat of losing his family, being shunned by the church, and learning to pay the bills on his own? Again, no.

It was the truth that set Tom free.

The enemy tried to convince Tom that his identity was connected to his sin. The only way Tom was going to experience true change was for him to realize that Christ in him was his true identity, not how others saw him or by how he performed. Tom's desire for porn could only be removed by replacing it with the truth that he was already complete in Christ. He didn't need another woman to make him feel better. Tom already had everything he'd ever need because the God of the universe dwells in him!

Untwisting the lies the enemy throws at us is like that old children's Christmas special *Rudolph the Red-Nosed Reindeer,* in which Herbie the dentist pulls teeth out of the abominable snowman. After that, the only thing the monster was good for was using his enormous size to put a star on top of the Christmas tree! The fear he'd generated by his huge, sharp teeth had been dismembered and removed. When you take the time to identify the lies the enemy has been throwing at you and replace them with what's true, you've just declawed the enemy. It's game over for Satan.

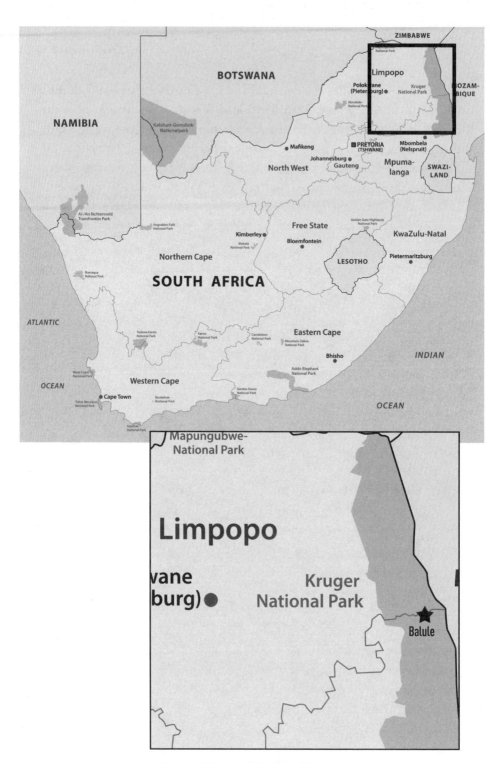

Kruger National Park and Balule

THE WILDS

AFRICA'S BIG FIVE

Something you have to learn in life is that you can't run away from your feelings. Whether they are feelings of fear, destructive thoughts, lustful ideas, or simply anger and resentment, if you try to run away, they will chase you up a tree, and leave you stranded with no way out. You have to face the things that you are feeling and deal with them. We are well aware that the way men think and the way women think are two completely different things. Many women sigh with delight when they see a deer. Most men only feel hunger. Most women tend to wear their feelings on their sleeves, open and exposed, while most men bury their feelings in a hole deep enough to reach China to avoid opening up. However, if men would learn to look at their emotions and stop running away, it would be a lot easier to face all of the tough issues they don't enjoy talking about. Like capturing a wild animal, you have to learn to quickly take your emotions captive in the wild before they come back and bite you. It's vital for you to learn to follow the trail of your emotions instead of running from them. I had to learn to track my emotions just like tracking dangerous game in the wild.

One of my favorite things to do in the wilderness is to sit around a campfire sharing and listening to hair-raising stories—men describing, in animated fashion, unbelievable, over-the-edge survival tales in which they faced and defeated death with the deck stacked against them. I've been in situations in which I've been afraid, but nothing is as scary to me as facing one of Africa's Big Five. As I've said before, everything in Africa either wants to stick you or kill you, so for those of us who love adventure, sitting around a campfire listening to the stories of African guides is as "over the top" as it gets.

Remember the snakes I told you about on my safari? That black mamba and the hero shot? Well, those snakes are definitely one of my personal Big Five, but let's talk about some of the other ones.

As I mentioned before, I spent time traipsing around in Kruger National Park with a couple of my adventure buddies before that safari. On our second day in Kruger, we pulled into a roadside gas station and outdoor café for fuel and some South African cuisine. It didn't take long for some of the local tree-dwellers to make their way towards our table to try and snatch our personal items or any food left unattended.

If you've never spent time around monkeys, you may think they are cute, cuddly creatures that want to sit in your lap and act just like Curious George, a fictitious children's book character. In reality, monkeys in the wild are curious, but they are also extremely dangerous. Baboons, for instance, have canine teeth over two inches long and have been known to take down a leopard when challenged.

Within minutes of noticing us, the monkeys began checking us out, and one was brave enough to come right up to our table. Thinking it was a good idea, and not seeing the "don't feed the monkeys sign," my friend, Ralph, tossed one of them a piece of his sandwich. Before Ralph could take his next breath, the manager of the diner began shouting at him from across the patio, calling him a stupid American and chasing the monkey away. After he calmed down, the manager explained to us that you *never* trust monkeys. Just the day before, a tourist had his throat ripped open by a monkey, an incident that threatened to curb the tourism traffic to his café.

Why do they attack humans who feed them? Well, monkeys have an eating hierarchy. First, the alpha male eats; next, the older family members eat; then, finally, the youngest ones. By giving a monkey your food, you are exhibiting weakness and inferiority, and he *will* attack you when the food runs out.

Later that afternoon, we arrived at a small satellite camp called Balule, a place of exquisite vistas deep in the heart of the park. Balule lies close to the mighty Olifants River, and is named after the Tsonga word for "buffalo." This camp is one of the best places for adventure seekers to experience nature firsthand and up close...very close.

As we rounded the final bend in the road leading into Balule, our headlights illuminated the bridge ahead of us, which was covered with dozens of monkeys. It kind of reminded me of the scene in *The Wizard of Oz* in which the flying monkeys dismember the scarecrow. That scene has always freaked me out. It quickly became apparent that something had spooked the monkeys, causing them to run away from the direction in which we were headed. It was very disquieting.

Balule is a place with only the most basic of facilities and no electricity—a low fence was the only barrier separating us from the wilderness. After we set up our three-man tent only feet from the eight-foot-tall chain-link fence, the sun began setting in the western sky, so we quickly made a makeshift table, started a small ironwood fire, and began preparing an evening meal. There's something to the wilderness experience, especially cooking over an open fire and hearing the distant roar of lions—I'd never felt so alive in my life.

As darkness closed in around us, I was just finishing a flame-broiled burger when I spotted a large pair of golden eyes floating some three feet off the ground and staring at me. The flickering of the fire reflected the ominous stare from the opposite side of the fence not ten yards away. Feeling somewhat protected in the wire enclosure, I moved toward the fence. Whatever it was didn't budge. Needing to relieve myself, I proceeded to do so through the wire fence before moving back to my position near the fire. Not thirty seconds later, a large spotted hyena approached, and relieved himself in the exact same spot. This was his territory, and he wanted me to know it. This behavior turned into a dominance game that the two of us maintained as long as the fluids were flowing. The spotted hyena has the strongest jaws in the animal kingdom, even stronger than a lion's. Even so, they stay clear of lions, especially male lions. I was going to stay on my side of the fence and clear of both of them!

THE TALE OF HARRY WOLHUTER

Before heading to bed, we sat around the ironwood fire retelling life-and-death stories, but this night, one story in particular came to mind. It was the story of a park ranger named Harry Wolhuter. Near the turn of the twentieth century, Harry had been attacked by two hungry lions on the prowl in almost the same spot we were sleeping. The following morning, we packed up, and headed to the main Kruger National Park camp at Skukuza. I was excited to get underway as there is a display there that documents Harry's amazing story of survival. Harry Wolhuter was the first game ranger hired by the Transvaal Republic (early name of the South African Republic) to range over the Sabi Game Reserve. His story is one of Kruger Park's most famous tales.

In August 1903, Wolhuter was riding on horseback along what is today the Lindanda Road, when two lions attacked him shortly after nightfall. The following is a segment in Harry's own words from his book, *Memories of a Game Ranger*:

> I heard a running rustle in the grass approaching me. I was still riding quietly along when two forms loomed up within three or four yards, and these I now recognized as two lions, and their behaviour was such I had little doubt but that their intentions were to attack my horse. Although, of course, I had my rifle (without which I never moved in the veld) there was not time to shoot, and as I hastily pulled my horse around I dug the spurs into his flanks in a frantic effort to urge him to his best speed to get away in time; but the approaching lion was already too close, and before the horse could get into its stride I felt a terrific impact behind me as the lion alighted on the horse's hindquarters.
>
> What happened next, of course, occupied only a few seconds, but I vividly recall the unpleasant sensation of expecting the crunch of the lion's jaws in my person. However, the terrified horse was bucking and plunging so violently that the lion was unable to maintain its hold, but it managed to knock me out of the saddle. Fortune is apt to act freakishly at all times, and it may seem a strange thing to suggest that it was fortunate for myself that I happened to fall almost on top of the second lion as he was running round in front of my horse, to get hold of it by the head. Had I fallen otherwise, however, it is probable that the lion would have

grasped me by the head. Actually, the eager brute gripped my right shoulder between its jaws and started to drag me away, and as it did so I could hear the clatter of my horse's hooves over the stony ground as it raced away with the first lion in hot pursuit; itself in turn being chased by my dog "Bull."

Meanwhile, the lion continued dragging me towards the neighbouring Metsimetsi Spruit. I was dragged along on my back, being held by my right shoulder, and as the lion was walking over me his claws would sometimes rip wounds in my arms and I was wearing a pair of spurs with strong leather straps, and these acted as brakes, scoring deep furrows in the ground over which we travelled. When the "brakes" acted too efficiently the lion would give an impatient jerk of his great head, which added excruciating pain to my shoulder, already deeply lacerated by the powerful teeth. I certainly was in a position to disagree emphatically with Dr. Livingstone's theory, based on his own personal experience, that the resulting shock from the bite of a large carnivorous animal so numbs the nerves that it deadens all the pain; for, in my own case, I was conscious of great physical agony; and in addition to this was the mental agony as to what the lion would presently do with me; whether he would kill me first or proceed to dine off me while I was still alive!

Of course, in those first few moments I was convinced that it was all over with me and that I had reached the end of my earthly career.

But then, as our painful progress still continued, it suddenly struck me that I might still have my sheath knife! I always carried this attached to my belt on the right side. Unfortunately, the knife did not fit too tightly in its sheath, and on two previous occasions when I had had a spill from my horse while galloping after game during the Boer War it had fallen out. It seemed almost too much to expect that it could still be safely there after the recent rough episodes. It took me some time to work my left hand round my back as the lion was dragging me over the ground, but eventually I reached the sheath, and, to my indescribable joy, the knife was still there! I secured it, and wondered where best first to stab the lion. It flashed through my mind that, many years ago, I had read in a magazine or newspaper that if you hit a cat on the nose he must sneeze before doing anything. This particular theory is, of course, incorrect; but at the time I seriously entertained the idea of attempting it, though on second thoughts I dismissed the notion, deciding that in any case he would just sneeze and pick me up again—this time perhaps in a more vital spot!

I decided finally to stick my knife into his heart, and so I began to feel very cautiously for his shoulder. The task was a difficult and complicated one because, gripped as I was, high up in the right shoulder, my head pressed right up against the lion's mane, which exuded a strong smell (incidentally, he was purring very loudly, something after the fashion of a cat—only on a far louder scale— perhaps in pleasant anticipation of the meal he intended to have) and this necessitated my reaching with my left hand holding the knife across his chest so as to gain access to his left shoulder. Any bungling, in this maneuver, would arouse the lion, with instantly fatal results to myself!

However, I managed it successfully, and knowing where his heart was located, I struck him twice, in quick succession, with two backhanded strokes behind the left shoulder. The lion let out a furious roar, and I desperately struck him again: this time upwards into his throat. I think this third thrust severed the jugular vein, as the blood spurted out in a stream all over me. The lion released his hold and slunk off into the darkness. Later I measured the distance, and found that he had dragged me sixty yards. Incidentally, it transpired later that both first thrusts had reached the heart.

The scene, could anyone have witnessed it, must have been eerie in the extreme, as, in the darkness, I staggered to my feet, not realizing how seriously I had wounded the lion, whose long-drawn moans resounded nearby. I thought first to frighten him off with human voice and shouted after him all the names I could think of, couched in the most lurid language. Suddenly I remembered the other lion that had chased my horse. It was more likely that it would fail to catch the horse, once the latter was at a full gallop, and then, what was more probable, it would return to its mate and find me there, quite unarmed except for my knife—as of course my rifle had been flung into the long grass when I fell off my horse.

At first I thought of setting the grass alight to keep away the second lion; and, getting the matchbox from my pocket, I gripped it in my teeth, as of course my right arm was quite useless, not only on account of the wound from the lion's teeth in my shoulder, but also because its claws had torn out some of the tendons about the wrist. I struck a match and put it to the grass, but as there was by now a heavy dew and the grass would not burn—fortunately, of course, as it turned out, else my rifle would have been burnt.

My next idea was to climb into a tree and thus place myself beyond the lion's reach. There were several trees in the vicinity, but they all had long stems, and with my one arm I was unable to climb them. Presently, however, I located one with a fork near the ground, and after a great deal of trouble I managed to climb into it, reaching a bough, some twelve feet from the ground, in which I sat. I was now commencing to feel very shaky indeed, both as a result of the shock I had sustained, and loss of blood; and what clothes I had left covering me were saturated with blood, both my own and that of the lion, and the effect of the cold night air on the damp clothing considerably added to my discomfort, while my shoulder was still bleeding badly. I realized that I might faint, from loss of blood, and fall off the bough on which I was sitting, so I removed my belt and somehow strapped myself to the tree. My thirst was terrible; and I would have offered much for a cup of water. One consoling reflection was that I knew my boys would find me as I was not far from the path.

Meanwhile I could still occasionally hear the lion I had stabbed grunting and groaning in the darkness, somewhere close by; and presently, resounding eerily over the night air, I heard the long-drawn guttural death-rattle in his throat—and felt a trifle better then as I knew I had killed him. My satisfaction was short-lived; however, as very soon afterwards approaching rustles in the grass heralded the arrival of the second lion, which, as I had surmised, had failed to catch my horse. I heard it approach the spot where I had got to my feet and from there, following my blood-spoor all the time, it advanced to the tree in which I sat. Arriving at the base of the tree, it reared itself up against the trunk and seemed to be about to try to climb it. I was overcome with horror at this turn of affairs, as it appeared as if I had got away from one lion, only to be caught by the other: the tree which harboured me being quite easy to climb (had it not been so I could never have worked my way up to my perch), and not absolutely beyond the powers of a determined, hungry lion! In despair I shouted down at the straining brute, whose upward-turned eyes I could momentarily glimpse reflected in the starlight, and this seemed to cause him to hesitate.

Fortunately, just then, my faithful dog "Bull" appeared on the scene. Never was I more grateful at the arrival of man or beast! He had evidently discovered that I was no longer on the horse, and was missing, and had come back to find me. I called to him, and encouraged him to go for the lion, which he did in right good heart, barking furiously at it and so distracting its attention that it made a short rush at the plucky dog, who managed to keep his distance.

And so this dreadful night passed on. The lion would leave the tree and I could hear him rustling about in the grass, and then he would return, and the faithful "Bull" would rush at him barking, and chase him off, and so on. Finally, it seemed to lie up somewhere in the neighbouring bush.

Some considerable time later, perhaps an hour, I heard a most welcome sound: the clatter of tin dishes rattling in a hamper on the head of one of my boys who was at last approaching along the path. In the stillness of the night one can hear the least sound quite a long way off in the veld. I shouted to him to beware, as there was a lion somewhere near. He asked me what he ought to do and I told him to climb into a tree. I heard a rattling crash, as he dropped the hamper, and then silence for a while. I then asked him if he was up a tree, and whether it was a big one: to which he replied that it was not a tall tree but that he had no wish to come down and search for a better one as he could already hear the lion rustling in the grass near him! He informed me that the other boys were not so far behind, and I then told him all that had happened—a recital of events which, to judge by the tone of his comments, did little to reassure him of the pleasantness of his present situation! After a time, which seemed ages, we heard the little pack of donkeys approaching along the path, and I shouted instructions to the boys to halt where they were, as there was a lion in the grass quite near, and to fire off a few shots to scare him. This they did, then as they approached to the tree in which I sat, I told them first of all to make a good fire, which did not take long to flare up, as some form of protection in case the lion returned: and then they assisted me down from the tree. It was a painful and laborious business, as I was very stiff and sore from my wounds, and I found the descent very much harder than the ascent.[7]

After resting a day, Harry was carried in a litter to receive medical assistance. The party arrived at Komatipoort four days later. Wolhuter was patched up by a doctor and then sent by train to Barberton Hospital, where he stayed for several weeks.

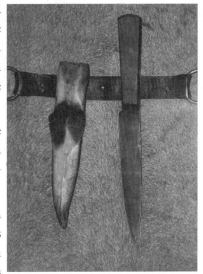

The knife Harry Wohutter used to kill the lion.

Harry's story was always an inspiring one to me that I tried to remember in tough times. He fought to survive and dodged every flaming arrow that was thrown at him.

I was awakened at around one o'clock in the morning to the sound of a pride of lions roaring ferociously in the darkness, along with the trumpeting of a single elephant. The lions had isolated a young elephant, and the adult female elephant was attempting to drive the lions away from her calf. Throughout the night, we were awakened by the

7. Harry Wolhuter, *Memories of a Game Ranger* (Johannesburg: Wildlife Protection Society of South Africa, 1948), quoted in Pat Hopkins and Bridget Hilton-Barber (compilers), *Worst Journeys: An anthology of South African travel disasters* (Zebra, 2005), 87–92.

bloodcurdling screams from a troop of baboons as a leopard on the hunt passed beneath their tree.

Just knowing Africa's Big Five was just on the other side of the eight-foot-tall fence kept our thoughts and emotions running in overdrive mode most of the night.

Note: In 1902, Harry Wolhuter was one of the first game rangers in the Sabi Nature Reserve, which would eventually, along with the Shingwedzi Nature Reserve, become the Kruger National Park. Originally a hunter, Wolhuter made the protection of the Kruger's wildlife his life's work. *Memories of a Game Ranger* tells of his days in the bush, when rangers went on horseback and lions considered them fair game. There was little in the way of danger Harry didn't have to cope with—from crocodiles in swimming holes to irate hippos at ranger posts—and that's not even taking into account the poachers, malaria, or the little old ladies wanting protection from those fearsome giraffes. Harry Wolhuter, born in 1876, was a legendary ranger in the Kruger National Park, and completed forty-four years of service before retiring in 1948. Today, the Lindanda Memorial marks the spot where he killed the lion, and the lion's pelt is still on display in the Stevenson-Hamilton Library in Skukuza. Wolhuter died in 1964.

5

MAN TEA

For the word of God is alive and active. Sharper than any double-edged sword, it penetrates even to dividing soul and Spirit, joints and marrow; it judges the thoughts and attitudes of the heart. (Hebrews 4:12)

A big part of dodging those flaming arrows and learning who you are in Christ is all about those emotions that I talked about at the beginning of the Wilds in this section. It is so tough for men to reveal their emotions that it's going to take the next two chapters and more for many of you to work through it. I know that talking about feelings is pretty much the last thing that guys want to do. We are tough, we like to go unshaven, we lift weights, we blow things up, and we go to the bathroom outside, but discussing emotions can be like Superman getting too close to kryptonite—we're afraid it makes us weak.

Little boys are taught early to associate their penises with a weapon or a sword, and it becomes a key component of their "manliness." Throughout adolescence, they pursue manhood in a variety of healthy and unhealthy ways. As boys grow into men, not much changes as we figuratively compare our manhood to see who's bigger, faster, or stronger when it comes to sports or business or romance. Men love competition, and can quickly get in touch with their anger, but connecting with other seemingly "less than masculine" emotions can be nearly impossible. It's time to lay Rambo aside and get real.

It's much easier to just keep quiet when we have a thought that isn't so great. It's even easier to channel our angry outbursts into inanimate objects—punching or kicking the wall, smashing breakable objects, or slamming doors. In fact, I'm suspect that a woman somewhere in the world is laughing because she invented those springy things that automatically close doors specifically for times when men don't want to talk about their emotions.

Today, however, we are going to get down-and-dirty, take it to the mat, and drink some "TEA." Bear with me, here. This is man TEA, so there won't be any finger sandwiches or sugar-coated pastries involved. This is rough, tough, burly, rumble-it-up manly TEA. So let's put Stallone on the shelf for a few minutes, grab your snot rags, raise your glass, make a toast, and get ready to rumble with our emotions!

MAN TEA

Having healthy (T) thoughts, (E) emotions, and (A) actions plays a pivotal role in survival situations. Losing your cool can spell disaster in a single heartbeat and leave you terrified and terrorized. In this chapter, we will learn how God's truth can turn fear into focus and remove the enemy's claws from us. You may not think about having TEA in the jungle, but the analogy can really help you out if you are in a place where you feel like you might start to get over-emotional.

Remember Harry Wolhuter from the story you just read? The guy who almost became supper for a hungry lion? The thing that strikes me the most about him wasn't that he survived the attack; it's that somehow he was able to kill the lion while he was being dragged away for dinner, all the while knowing that if he didn't act quickly, the lion's breath would soon smell like him! Obviously, the lion was much larger and stronger than Harry, but Harry had something on the inside the lion didn't take into consideration. Harry's *thoughts* are what made him so dangerous.

If there's one thing I like, it's a great cup of coffee first thing in the morning. Years ago, a man named Dale, who worked in our building, would come into my office every day, open up his Thermos of freshly-ground coffee, offer me a hot cup, and then share some current event. That's how our conversations usually got started.

One particular morning, I'd had someone bring me in a hot cup of flavored tea before Dale got to my office. When he came in and was about to pour me a cup of his special brew, I said, "Thanks, Dale, but I already have a cup of flavored tea."

Dale looked at me and replied, "Flavored tea? Real men don't drink flavored tea!"

I thought for a moment, then replied, "Dale, real men drink anything they want!"

Making a pot of hot coffee over a glowing campfire is one of my favorite things to do. The evening my friends and I were camping south of the Oliphant's River at Balule (the very spot where Harry Wolhuter's lion attack occurred), one of my friend's skills as a chef kicked in. As our ironwood fire lowered to a flicker, he placed a pot of hot water above the flames, opened a Ziploc baggie he'd brought along, and poured the ingredients into the boiling water. This was his special adventure tea, made only for a time like this. I laughed and told the "real men don't drink flavored tea" story. I guess the truth is that it matters more what a man thinks than what he drinks. We named this fireside beverage "MAN T-E-A." This Man Tea (T-E-A) would later become an acronym for Thoughts, Emotions, and Actions, a discipleship and counseling tool my mentor Derek Wilder had taught me several years earlier, used in helping me to renew my mind. T-E-A is a key weapon in the offensive battle we wage against Satan.

So, what's in Man TEA? I can tell you this much: it's not really what's in the Man TEA that counts, but rather what's in the man. One of the biggest problems men face is that we have been taught the opposite. We are taught that it's what we put out—money, ideas, super-talented children, or some sort of successful business venture—that defines our success, both in life and as a Christian. It's unrealistic to put so much pressure on ourselves. We are not going to hit a hole-in-one every time we swing. It's just not going to happen. Our thinking has been corrupted. We've bought into the lie that suggests that what people see on the outside is who we are. Lucky for us, Jesus focuses on something different. He is more concerned with what is *inside* a man than with his *outward* actions.

In Mark 7, Jesus confronted some Pharisees, who were the most numerous and influential of the religious Jews of Jesus' day. They were legalists, and they always wanted the limelight. Jesus' "naughty" disciples had just eaten without washing their hands. The hand-washing was a tradition passed down by Jewish elders and one of 614 man-made Jewish laws.

The Pharisees criticized Jesus' disciples for not keeping their traditions. Jesus got in their faces and called them hypocrites. He told them they were more concerned about eating etiquette than with what came out of their mouths. Then He suggested that what comes out of your mouth is the real problem, not what you're putting in it.

> *You don't get wormy apples off a healthy tree, nor good apples off a diseased tree. The health of the apple tells the health of the tree. You must begin with your own life-giving lives. It's who you are, not what you say and do, that counts. Your true being brims over into true words and deeds.* (Luke 6:43–45 MSG)

The *"who you are"* is the focus here; Christ in you. If your roots are secure in your true identity, you will bear *"healthy"* fruit, because your true being, God's Spirit in you, will brim over into true words and deeds. When we forget who we are or are deceived into believing our identity comes from our performance or another person's opinion of us, we will produce wormy, *"diseased"* fruit. When we learn to put God's thoughts into our minds, healthy emotions and actions will come out.

Let's create a fictional situation where we can see the options to maintain healthy thoughts that can produce positive actions instead of negativity and an "I suck" mentality:

Ron and Cheryl were experiencing an intimacy problem. They hadn't been physically close for months. Cheryl felt that Ron had been insensitive towards her feelings about the importance of having a date night, and Ron felt Cheryl hadn't understood his sexual needs as a man and had been withholding intimacy from him. Every night, Ron would try to move toward Cheryl, which always resulted in her bringing up how she wanted to be "dated" first. Ron always had an excuse: he'd been too busy or there wasn't enough money in their budget. This couple was at a stalemate, and both were withholding love from each other.

One day, Ron was on the computer while his wife was out for an evening with the girls. Ron was a huge Dallas Cowboys fan and, at first, he was simply looking at the team's homepage. On an advertisement on the sidebar, Ron noticed a scantily-clothed cheerleader. He thought, *Wow, she's beautiful! I wonder if a woman like that would want me or treat me the way my wife does.*

Before Ron knew what was happening, he clicked the mouse, and slowly began to be dragged into a dangerous place. Before he knew it, he'd been clicking on images and videos for two hours. It's like his mind became totally clouded, and he now was openly searching for a way to see more of what he wasn't getting at home. What Ron didn't know was that the images and videos embedded on the pages were like the lions hiding in the tall grass, waiting to snare Harry Wolhuter. Other eyes were watching both men, and neither was able to anticipate the potential harm awaiting them.

Cheryl was having a great time with the girls. They talked about kids, jobs, and, of course, relationships. Cheryl knew someone would eventually ask about how she and Ron were getting along, and then it happened.

"Cheryl, so how are you and Ron doing?"

Cheryl paused, swallowed hard, and replied, "Well, if you like living without being pursued, then I guess we're doing great!"

Now all eyes were on Cheryl.

"Cheryl, why are you staying in that relationship if it's so bad?"

Cheryl responded, "I don't believe in divorce. I don't think it's something God would want. I just wish he'd want to date me."

About that time, Cheryl's friend Denise spoke up. "You know what I do when my husband isn't pursuing or passionate towards me? I go and get a romance novel or rent some steamy video, curl up on the couch, and disappear into my own fantasy world. No harm, no foul!"

At the end of the dinner, the girls parted ways. Cheryl remembered what Denise had said. She knew going into a fantasy world wasn't where God wanted her to go, but her emotions were fraught from wishing that Ron would do more to court her.

As she drove past the corner bookstore, she looked at her watch. She still had an hour left before she had to be home. She pulled in the parking lot, grabbed her checkbook, and walked in. Within twenty minutes, she'd found a steamy romance novel, and was turning its pages as fast as her fingers could fly. *If only my husband would treat me like this,* Cheryl thought.

The enemy now had his claws buried deep into the minds of Ron and Cheryl, and the lies they'd bought into were dragging them farther away from who they really were. Their thoughts (*I deserve better*) were causing unhealthy emotions (anger and lust), which now had led to unhealthy actions. If neither Cheryl nor Ron were able to find reverse, they were both heading off a cliff.

While I was having a lunch appointment with a buddy, he brought up the very sensitive topic of pornography. Most of the conversations I have with men around the subject of porn are inevitably outside the church walls, mostly because of the shame and condemnation religious institutions have attached to that particular sin. My friend had been on a fishing trip with a group of guys from our church, and they had begun to discuss this taboo topic. One of the men had been riding with his wife in their car when she brought up the topic of pornography. You can guess how the conversation went when she began by saying, "I can't believe that men look at this stuff! They're pigs. It's so disgusting. I feel violated when I see images of scantly clothed women on TV and in magazines. It makes me feel ugly and worthless. I can't compete with those images."

Then she directed her words toward her husband: "If you want those type of women, you can have them! If I ever catch you looking at that trash, you can just pack up your stuff and get out because I won't put up with it!"

No doubt, this is a sensitive topic and for good reasons. But, if you look closely, you'll see that her emotions were driven by what she was thinking. Look at these two sentences from her tirade:

- "I feel violated when I see images of beautiful, scantly clothed women on TV and in magazines."
- "It makes me feel ugly and worthless."

While we all know that God doesn't want you staring at porn, this guy's wife was buying in to the idea that only specific women are beautiful. Her disdain was not over the fact that the half-naked women could possibly cause her husband to have a lustful thought; it was over the fact that they made her feel insecure. The wife was thinking (T) that she was less than these other women, emotional (E) because she began to feel insecure, and her actions (A) were to dig into her husband using shame and fear to control a behavior he had not even exhibited. When the enemy started pouring his lies into her Man Tea, the results became toxic.

What weapon can we use to reverse his deadly arrows? Take a look at this passage from 2 Corinthians 10:5. It is a key verse to lock and load.

We demolish arguments and every pretension [claim] that sets itself up against the knowledge of God, and we take captive every thought to make it obedient to Christ.

The key to that verse is *"we take captive every thought to make it obedient to Christ."* This is the beginning of dismantling and demolishing the lies of the one who is trying to kill us. But, as you will see in the next chapter, this is not something we can do alone.

Emotions, in and of themselves, are not bad. God gave them to us. Those emotions are letting us know if what we are thinking is healthy or unhealthy so we can deal with them.

Let's see how Cheryl could have confronted the enemy's lies if she had detected his hand.

STEP 1 – IDENTIFY THE UNHEALTHY EMOTION

Cheryl could do this by taking her spiritual temperature. She could try to identify her emotions by putting the words "I feel" before them. For example, "I feel happy. I feel loved. I feel content."

Healthy emotions line up with the fruit of the Spirit: *"Love, joy, peace, forbearance [patience], kindness, goodness, faithfulness, gentleness and self-control"* (Galatians 5:22–23).

Unhealthy emotions line up with the deeds of the flesh, things like fear, worry, doubt, rage, fits of anger, lust, and shame. For example, "I feel angry. I feel jealous. I feel anxious. I feel lustful." (See Galatians 5:19–21.)

STEP 2 – IDENTIFY THE UNHEALTHY THOUGHT

How could Cheryl do this? She could take every thought captive, according to Paul's words in 2 Corinthians. If her thoughts are causing unhealthy emotions, you can bet that Satan is using his flaming arrows, like past and future thinking:

+ *He used to pursue me and that made me feel wanted.*

+ *What if he never treats me the way I want to be treated? Then what?*

Cheryl has to choose to proactively take control of the unhealthy thought and write it down so she can clearly see the thought in front of her. If it lines up with the deeds of the flesh, she can know with confidence that a lie is twisted up somewhere around the roots of her thoughts. She can identify this lie by moving into Step 3.

STEP 3 - IDENTIFY THE TRUTH

Cheryl takes the unhealthy thought captive by untwisting the lies she's buying into by holding them up against the light of God's truth. For example, consider the lie: "I would feel better about myself if my husband courted me like he did when we were dating."

Now consider the truth: *My worth and value have nothing to do with my husband's opinions of me or whether he moves toward me. I am already deeply loved and 100 percent complete because Christ dwells in me!*

We know that the enemy loves to use condemnation to make us feel afraid, ashamed, and not good enough. Because those emotions line up with the deeds of the flesh, we can identify the lie we're buying into by looking at the thought and replacing it with God's truth: *"Therefore, there is now no condemnation for those who are in Christ Jesus"* (Romans 8:1).

STEP 4 - RENEW YOUR MIND

Identifying the truth isn't enough; Cheryl must also renew her mind with that truth. Keep writing it down. Memorize it. Put it on a mirror. Whatever it takes!

Romans 12: 2 says that you are to *"be transformed by the renewing of your mind."* If Cheryl doesn't do step 4, nothing else will change.

TRACKING THE TRANSFORMATION OF THE MIND

A great exercise to track the transformation that occurs through the renewing of the mind is to take a thought and write down the percentage you believe the initial thought to be true. Do you believe the thought is 75 percent true? Fifty percent true? Twenty percent true?

Then, after untwisting your thought from God's truth and renewing your mind for several days, revisit that percentage. Has it gone down?

For example, Cheryl could go back to an earlier thought and write down the percentage she now believes the unhealthy thought to be true. Example: *I should be feeling shame and condemnation after I read that steamy romance novel.*

But there is a huge difference between *condemnation* and *conviction.* Condemnation attempts to use shame to promote change, but it only leaves the sinner feeling worse, because it robs them of their identity of being "in Christ." However, conviction is an inner prompting from the Holy Spirit toward obedience. Conviction focuses on God and what He wants, while condemnation focuses on us and how bad we are. Conviction ultimately moves us toward what God wants. Condemnation chases us further away from what God wants through fear and shame.

For instance, conviction may lead Cheryl to repent and apologize to make things right with her husband. Condemnation might lead her to act out through overeating, binge drinking, or reading more steamy books because she feels bad about herself. She does this because she's trying to relieve the painful thought of condemnation: that she is "a horrible person." Condemnation is a powerful trick the enemy loves to use because he knows you'll be prompted toward sin, in search of relief from the pressure you are feeling. But such relief is only a momentary fix that leaves you feeling even more ashamed and condemned afterward.

We have to remember one last thing that is important about Ron and Cheryl's situation. While the flaming arrows of doubt were flying at Cheryl, she began to feel angry, unworthy, unappreciated, and every other thought that wives and mothers experience at some point in their marriages and family lives. Satan was spitting lies at her as fast as a poison dart frog, and she believed them. While Cheryl is feeling all those emotions bubble to the surface, Ron is stuffing his feelings down, and listening to the inner thoughts that are telling him how undesirable he is. He's not the young stallion that he once was. Maybe that's why Cheryl isn't interested in a more sexual relationship. She used to want him all of the time, back when they had no kids, and he had more time to go to the gym. Ron locks those emotions away, and decides it's easier to look at an intangible woman who will never put him down and won't make him talk about what he is feeling. If he'd only drank a little bit of Man Tea, opened up to his wife, and tell her how he is feeling, he may get lucky enough to enjoy some alone time with a real woman—his wife.

Dealing with your emotions is like having a life preserver when you're drowning. If you refuse to look at your emotions, they will become like an anchor tied around your neck, pulling you into a deep, dark, cold sea of isolation and resentment, where you will most certainly slip into spiritual hypothermia.

INTO THE WILDS FIELD GUIDE

CHAPTER FIVE: MAN TEA

For the word of God is alive and active. Sharper than any double-edged sword, it penetrates even to dividing soul and spirit, joints and marrow; it judges the thoughts and attitudes of the heart. (Hebrews 4:12)

Asking a man to get in touch with his emotions is about as difficult as herding cats. As soon as we ask men to do that, the room clears. But this is where we separate the men from the boys. This is the dangerous truth every man needs to know, not only to survive the wilds, but more importantly, to survive the home front, where life happens every day.

One of the main reasons men don't like to talk about how they're feeling is because it makes them feel weak, like they don't have what it takes. Nothing could be further from the truth. You *do* have what it takes "in Christ," but not if you live out of your own strength. God will allow you to attempt to live by your own striving so that you can experience an important life revelation: you can't go it alone. You need brothers, and, more importantly, *you need a Savior.*

Having healthy (T) thoughts, (E) emotions, and (A) actions play pivotal roles in survival situations. Losing your cool can spell disaster in a single heartbeat, leaving you terrified and terrorized. It's time to draw our weapon and head into the wilds.

1. As lion slobber was running down Harry Wolhutter's face, and he realized that the big cat's breath was going to smell like him if he didn't take action, what emotions do you think he was experiencing?

2. What enabled Harry, while still in the mouth of the lion, to take action and plunge the sheath knife deep into the lion's chest? (Optional ice breaker: Have the men try to say "sheath knife" five times fast.)

3. What is your biggest fear and why?

4. What might happen if you risked doing something different and stepped into that fear? What beliefs do you have that are holding you back?

Read the following verse aloud…

You don't get wormy apples off a healthy tree, nor good apples off a diseased tree. The health of the apple tells the health of the tree. You must begin with your own life-giving lives. It's who you are, not what you say and do, that counts. Your true being brims over into true words and deeds. (Luke 6:43–45 MSG)

Unhealthy thinking, which ultimately causes the production of unhealthy fruit, stems from where our roots are planted. It's what we truly *believe* (the roots) that shapes how we think, feel, and act (the fruit). Have you ever heard the old saying "garbage in, garbage out"? If we believe that our worth and value is derived from our performance, or from others' opinions of us, then those beliefs will only produce wormy apples—unhealthy thoughts—because they are rooted in lies. In order to produce healthy fruit, we must untangle the lies and replace them with the truth. How do we do that?

In Romans 12 and 2 Corinthinans 10, the Bible gives us a map detailing a clear plan for dismantling and demolishing the lies of the enemy.

*Do not conform to the pattern of this world, but **be transformed by the renewing of your mind**. Then you will be able to test and approve what God's will is—his good, pleasing and perfect will.* (Romans 12:2)

*We demolish arguments and every pretension that sets itself up against the knowledge of God, and **we take captive every thought** to make it obedient to Christ.* (2 Corinthians 10:5)

*We use our powerful God-tools for smashing warped philosophies, tearing down barriers erected against the truth of God, **fitting every loose thought and emotion and impulse** [action] **into the structure of life shaped by Christ.*** (2 Corinthians 10:5 MSG)

The apostle Paul instructed us to take every thought captive. But how? Romans 12:2 tells us not to conform to the pattern of this world, but to *"be transformed by the renewing of* [our] *mind."* Realizing that *"be transformed"* is in the passive voice lets me know it's not something I can do on my own, but only something that God can do. It's God's job, through the Holy Spirit, to do the *transforming*; it's my job to do the *renewing*.

The following exercise is an excellent tool for renewing your mind, and helping to line up your thoughts with God's truth. Untangling the lies of the enemy can be compared to trying to get that "bird's nest" out of your fishing line when it gets all tangled up. It can be so frustrating that you don't even know where to begin. I encourage you to read the example below.

Cheryl was buying into some destructive lies in her life. See how she untangled her thoughts and broke free of unhealthy thoughts, emotions, and actions (yes, women can have TEA also) caused by those lies.

STEP 1: IDENTIFY THE UNHEALTHY EMOTION

Cheryl took her "spiritual temperature." She did this by looking at her emotions. She identified each emotion by putting the words "I feel" before them. (Example: I feel happy. I feel loved. I feel content.)

Healthy emotions line up with the fruit of the Spirit: *"...love, joy, peace, patience, kindness, goodness, faithfulness, gentleness and self-control"* (Galatians 5:22–23 NLT).

Unhealthy emotions line up with the demands of the flesh, things like fear, worry, doubt, rage, fits of anger, lust, shame, etc. (Example: I feel angry. I feel jealous. I feel anxious. I feel lustful. (See Galatians 5:19–21.)

STEP 2: IDENTIFY THE UNHEALTHY THOUGHT

Cheryl had to take captive every thought, according to Paul's words in 2 Corinthians. If any of her thoughts were causing unhealthy emotions, you can bet that Satan was using them as flaming arrows to torment her with past and future thinking.

My husband used to pursue me and that made me feel wanted.

What if he never treats me the way I want to be treated? Then what?

Cheryl had to choose to proactively take control of the unhealthy thought and write it down. Then she was able to clearly see the thought in front of her. If her thoughts lined up with the deeds of the flesh in Galatians 5:19–25, she knew with confidence that a lie had entangled itself around the roots of her thoughts. She was able to identify this lie by moving on to Step 3.

STEP 3: IDENTIFY THE TRUTH

Cheryl was able to take the unhealthy thought captive by untwisting the lies and holding them up against the light of God's truth.

Example of thought lie: *I would feel better about myself if my husband courted me like he did when we were dating.*

Example of thought truth: *My worth and value have nothing to do with my husband's opinions of me, or whether or not he moves toward me. I am already deeply loved and 100 percent complete because Christ dwells in me!*

We know that the enemy loves to use condemnation to make us feel afraid, ashamed, and not good enough. Because those emotions line up with the deeds of the flesh, we can identify the lie we're buying into by looking at the thought, and by replacing the unhealthy thought with God's truth.

There is now no condemnation for those who are in Christ Jesus.

(Romans 8:1)

STEP 4: RENEW YOUR MIND

Simply identifying the truth isn't enough; Cheryl had to renew her mind with the truth. She had to keep writing it down, memorize it, and even stick it on her bathroom mirror. Whatever it takes!

NOTE: If you do not renew your mind with the truth, nothing changes!

THE FOUR STEPS

(Complete the following exercise)

1. Identify any unhealthy emotion(s) and write it/them down.

2. Identify any unhealthy thought(s) and write them down.

3. Identify the truth and write it down.

4. Renew your mind.

TRACK YOUR TRANSFORMATION

A great exercise to recognize transformation that's happening through the renewing of your mind is for you to write down the percentage you believe an initial thought to be true. After untwisting your thoughts with God's truth, and renewing your mind for several days, go back and look at the original thought. Write down the percentage you now believe the unhealthy thought to be true.

If you're struggling finding scriptures to help you get to the truth, you can go to www.menministry.org. Click on the "Truth Finder" at the top of the page, select a topic, and then click on "search." This is a great tool in helping you find the truth to assist you in untangling lies.

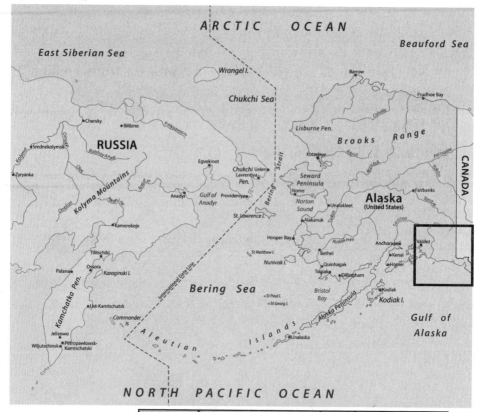

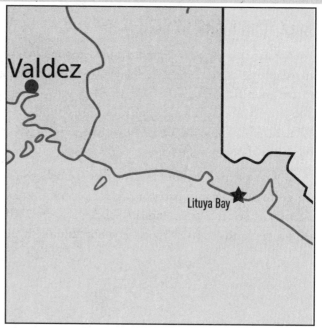

Lituya Bay Alaska

6

SPIRITUAL HYPOTHERMIA

When you don't understand the power of emotions, you are blind to the arrows, and you start to sink into a cold, dark, and almost unreachable place. It's as if you've slipped into a spiritual coma and lost your ability to communicate about what's happening on the inside. Not only do you push people away when you get to that point, but you unconsciously distance yourself from God, as well. Once you've reached a spiritual temperature below your breaking point, it's extremely hard to bounce back from the drop.

On July 9, 1958, one of the most remarkable events in recorded history occurred in a place called Lituya Bay, Alaska. A massive tsunami washed across the bay, wiping out everything in its path. At its peak, the wave reached 1,720 feet high, 250 feet higher than the Empire State Building. Entire forests were annihilated in its wake, and much of the land was stripped of soil down to the bedrock.

Lituya Bay is located in southwest Alaska. It consists of a narrow fjord approximately seven miles long and approximately two miles wide. On that day, just after 10 p.m., a magnitude 7.7 earthquake occurred on the Fairweather Fault, about twelve and a half miles from Lituya Bay. This ensuing catastrophic tsunami was the result of tectonic plates, drastically shifted by the earthquake, tilting the town of Lituya Bay toward the ocean. In addition to the wave, seismic waves also triggered a landslide that collapsed into the Lituya Bay fjord.

Lituya Bay is famous for hosting four recorded tsunamis over one hundred feet high: in 1854 (395 feet), 1899 (200 feet), 1936 (490 feet), and 1958 (1,720 feet).

There were three fishing boats anchored near the entrance of Lituya Bay on that fateful day. One boat sank and its crew was killed. The other two boats were able to ride the waves. Among the survivors were Adam Gray, William A. Swanson, and Howard G. Ulrich, who each provided accounts of what they observed. Based on Swanson's description of the length of time it took the wave to reach his boat after submerging Cenotaph Island near the bay's entrance, the wave may have been traveling at speeds up to 600 mph.

The immense power and devastation of tsunamis has been witnessed in recent years due to the increased number of public cameras in existence. Aerial and still-mounted cameras are on almost every helicopter, plane, ship, and city block. With the current explosion of smart phones, a huge portion of the world's population is able to capture live events and almost instantly post them on the Internet.

I will never forget watching the 2004 Indian Ocean tsunami that killed more than 230,000 people in fourteen countries. Disaster struck again seven years later in 2011 off the Pacific coast of the Tōhoku region of Japan, leaving 15,870 people dead, 6,114 injured, and 2,814 missing. Both of these catastrophic events were caused by earthquakes deep under the ocean floor. Debris from the Japanese tsunami is still washing ashore in Alaska.

While doing the research for this book, I came across a number of survivors' stories. A common theme was that they were so paralyzed by fear that it was all they could do to remember to swim. Tens of thousands didn't. Earthquakes are an unimaginable power that can transform entire landscapes and lives for generations.

We can suffer similar consequences when we are unable to determine where lies are coming from, and how to replace them with the truth. Just like we already learned in Man TEA, unhealthy thoughts cause unhealthy emotions that can paralyze us and distort our thinking, causing us to forget to swim toward better health. It's a humbling experience to be at nature's mercy. If you can't get your emotions in check and focus on healthy thoughts, you're dead. It's that simple. As told you earlier, I was seconds away from succumbing to hypothermia in Poison Pass. The healthy thoughts of the men who warmed me up probably saved my life.

WHEN LIES SEEP IN

In 1985, I was back in Alaska for a second time. I was working on a commercial fishing boat out of Bristol Bay, using gill nets to catch salmon. Gill nets are designed so that when the fish swims into its webbing, its head gets lodged, and it is unable to pull itself out. When we pulled the gill nets onto the boat, we would use a curved blade, something called a "fish pick," to pull the net from around the gills of the salmon. We freed the smaller fish that were not considered to be "keepers"; otherwise, the acceptable salmon remained trapped in the net.

Quality raingear is created to keep you dry and warm. If your raingear is faulty or springs a leak, you run the risk of getting hypothermia and making poor decisions. I had accidentally torn a hole in my rain suit with my fish pick. The icy-cold water pooled in my bootleg, soaking my pants, long johns, and wool socks, and caused my body temperature drop dramatically. Unbeknownst to me, I'd been working with the icy water trapped in my bootleg for six hours. Combine that with sweating profusely beneath my rubber raingear, and it was a cocktail for disaster.

Hypothermia occurs when our body core temperature drops below ninety-five degrees. As symptoms slowly set in, the victim usually remains unaware of their condition. Some of the telltale signs of hypothermia are:

+ Confusion or difficulty thinking
+ Poor decision-making, such as trying to remove warm clothes
+ Progressive loss of consciousness
+ Slurred speech or mumbling
+ Shivering
+ Clumsiness or lack of coordination
+ Stumbling
+ Drowsiness or low energy
+ Apathy or lack of concern about one's condition
+ Weak pulse
+ Slow, shallow breathing

One deadly aspect of hypothermia is that the victim's confused thinking leads to poor decision-making, and that can be the real problem. Hypothermia is a silent stalker.

Just as cold can be a relentless killer, so are the flaming arrows, or lies, that Satan shoots our way. At first, the targeted victim isn't aware they've been struck by the arrows, because, like the hole in my raingear, the arrows are small. If holes in raingear aren't detected and patched quickly, they grow larger and fill up with water faster. Likewise, if lies are not detected quickly, they grow larger and are able to do more damage. I call this process, "falling into spiritual hypothermia."

Lust has knocked a lot of good men down, and washed them out of the ministry. David, when tempted with Bathsheba, left himself unguarded. He allowed lies to take root in his mind. *She should be mine*, he thought. This is one of the oldest lies in the book! The "coveting lie" is wanting what you don't have, thinking, incorrectly, that somehow, if you can just get "it," you will find meaning, your life will have value, and you'll feel better about yourself. Those few moments David spent gazing at his neighbor's rooftop flooded his mind with unhealthy thoughts, creating unhealthy waves of emotion that knocked him off of his feet. David stopped swimming and sank into the cold arms of adultery.

Satan lights his arrows on fire, with the intent that the fire will spread. He doesn't merely lie to deceive us; he plans for the flames to overtake not only our feelings but our actions as well.

1. First, the thought: *I'd be happier with someone else.*

2. Then, the emotion: lust

3. Finally, the action: an affair (even if only an emotional one of the mind)

It can be a vicious cycle, set in motion by a heartless deceiver who doesn't care about vows, family, or even your life. He wants nothing more than to see you, and those closest to you, destroyed. When you succumb to those arrows, you slip into spiritual hypothermia faster than you thought was possible.

But aren't those kind of things "just going to happen" in a situation like that? It doesn't mean that I *believe* the lie if I only think those thoughts, does it? Wouldn't anyone think like that in a similar situation?

The apostle Paul classified anger, lust, jealousy, and impurity as *"acts of the flesh"* (Galatians 5:19). Jesus talked about deceit, slander, and pride as *"things that come out of a person's mouth.... For out of the heart come evil thoughts"* (Matthew 15:18, 19). He added, *"These are what defile a person"* (verse 20).

LIVING FROM THE INSIDE-OUT

That's the flipside of what I said before: it's what's inside of the man that counts.

> *A good man brings good things out of the good stored up in his heart, and an evil man brings evil things out of the evil stored up in his heart. For the mouth speaks what the heart is full of.* (Luke 6:45)

In effect, it's who you are, not what you say and do, that counts. Your true being brims over into true words and deeds. The good inside you produces good on the outside. Here in Luke, Jesus also warns that the bad inside you will also eventually bubble to the surface.

Jesus didn't mince words when it came to describing Satan. The devil, Jesus said, *"was a murderer from the beginning.... When he lies, he speaks his native language, for he is a liar and the father of lies"* (John 8:44).

When Satan lies, he lies to incite us. Lust should be a red flag in our lives, not because noticing a woman's beauty is wrong or unpleasant, but when noticing turns to "wanting what we don't have," that admiration turns to lust, and is pointing to something worse that exists within us.

Paul warned Titus about it:

> *At one time we too were foolish, disobedient, deceived and enslaved by all kinds of passions and pleasures. We lived in malice and envy, being hated and hating one another.* (Titus 3:3)

When we are angry, lustful, or jealous, it's simply the sound of a fire alarm. Identifying those unhealthy emotions is how we take our own spiritual temperature.

This is a big deal. These feelings come from deception, from the liar and the lies we believe.

> But the fruit of the Spirit is love, joy, peace, patience, kindness, goodness, faithfulness, gentleness, self-control; against such things there is no law. (Galatians 5:22–23)

When we are living from the inside-out, Christ's Spirit in us is our spiritual GPS. His fruits are healthy fruits. When we are thinking correctly, because our belief system is grounded in Him, our emotions line up with the fruit of the Spirit—love, peace, patience, kindness, goodness, faithfulness, gentleness, and self-control—and healthy actions result. If I think, *My wife's depression doesn't have the power over me to make me angry, and I don't need to have an affair because I am already 100 percent complete in Christ*, I am then free to choose not to be tyrannized by the lies of the enemy, and I can actually move toward my wife rather than away from her by disappearing to the garage, the golf course, or pornography, or by lashing out in anger. This only happens when I've renewed my mind and have sucked down a big 'ol gulp of Man Tea. I'm confronting my emotions openly and tackling them faster than a three-hundred-pound defensive end at the Super Bowl.

One of the most dangerous teachings I've seen concerning a man gazing at a woman was in a book that came out a few years ago. The author describes a technique to help curb a man's appetite for lusting after a beautiful woman by bouncing his eyes to other objects in the room so that he's not focused on the beauty in front of him. It's a form of behavior modification, or "fake it till you make it." No doubt, if a man is lusting after a beautiful woman, he needs to deal with the issue, but by "trying harder" or "eye bouncing," he's not dealing with the root cause, which is his desire for the woman to somehow make him more of a man if she responds to his gaze. Eye bouncing may deal with an unhealthy action, which is "rotten fruit," but you have to get to the root of the tree where the lies are growing. Men desire to look at beautiful woman, and God made women beautiful! They are His creation. It's the untamed desire of a man, wanting what he does not have, that's the issue.

If we say that looking at a woman in an unhealthy way, whether through porn or lusting, is a sin, which I agree it is, then we must admit that the opposite is true as well. If a man refuses to look at a beautiful woman because he feels condemned, afraid of God, or believes it makes him a better, more godly man, he's either walking in fear and shame of his actions, or his behavior becomes a source of pride and self-righteousness. Both are lies from the enemy. That's why the answer is not found merely in behavior, but in our thought life.

When I'm believing what's true about myself, that I'm already complete in Christ and my desires are met in Him, do I need to lust after some hot thing to make myself feel better? Behavior modification may play a small role in keeping myself from doing immediate damage, but ultimately, you have to deal with the core issue, which is: my identity is in Christ, not in what others think about me or in my performance. Focus on that truth! Let your thoughts bounce on that for a few minutes.

Paul's words to the church at Philippi are key:

Finally, brothers and sisters, whatever is true, whatever is noble, whatever is right, whatever is pure, whatever is lovely, whatever is admirable—if anything is excellent or praiseworthy—think about such things. (Philippians 4:8)

It's paramount that we understand our motivation in this: we don't trace our actions back to our emotions and then to our thoughts in order to create better behavior. We do it out of a desire to be completely God's on the inside, where it counts.

THE EMOTION THING

In Jesus' famous woman-at-the-well conversation, He said, "*A time is coming and has now come when the true worshipers will worship the Father in the Spirit and in truth, for they are the kind of worshipers the Father seeks*" (John 4:23).

Transformation isn't about bettering our behavior. It's about worship.

It's not always easy for a guy to relate to exactly what his emotions are trying to say. It can be confusing, and it will probably take a while before you completely let go and start being vocal about your emotions. But you will be freer and more content. Keeping all of that stuff inside of you will eat you alive, just like the parasites hidden in sparkling-clear Third-World water sources that hasn't been boiled. You need to boil the unhealthy thoughts and emotions out of you by renewing your mind, or you are going to be miserable.

Alaskan salmon can find their way back to their original spawning streams to give new life in the very environment in which they were hatched. No one knows exactly how it happens. Science has determined that their inner navigation system is a result of the magnetic poles, water temperature differences, and the polarization of light that results from the sun's angle in the sky. Researchers have learned that the smell of certain sediments causes them to return to the streams where they came from. Whatever the case may be, they are following an internal source that leads them back to the spot where their life was first formed. The same is true when we follow the Holy Spirit within us: it leads us back to our Creator. Drinking in Man Tea and replacing the enemy's lies with God's truth will keep you from slipping into spiritual hypothermia...I promise.

Once you've really got this emotion thing down, it's time to learn how to relate those emotions to others, which can be even harder than relating to them within yourself. The Big Five in Africa were terrifying, but the Big Five at home can be even scarier. You've got to boil the unhealthy emotions out of your mind and rehydrate with God's truth, or you are going to be miserable.

INTO THE WILDS FIELD GUIDE

CHAPTER SIX: SPIRITUAL HYPOTHERMIA

Hypothermia happens when our body's core temperature drops, causing our minds to shut down. One deadly aspect of hypothermia is that the confused thinking leads to poor decision-making, and many times that is what gets the victim in real trouble. Hypothermia is a silent killer. So is spiritual hypothermia.

When you don't understand the power of emotions, you are blind to the arrows, and you start to sink into a cold, dark, and almost unreachable place. It's as if you've slipped into a spiritual coma and lost your ability to communicate what's happening on the inside. When you get to such a place, not only do you push people away, but you also unconsciously distance yourself from God. Once you've reached a spiritual temperature below your breaking point, it's extremely hard to bounce back from the drop.

Cold can be a relentless, silent killer. So are the flaming arrows, or lies, that Satan shoots at us. At first, the targeted victim isn't aware they've been struck by the arrows, because the holes are small, like the hole in my rainsuit in this chapter. But if those holes aren't detected and patched quickly, they can grow larger, and your rainsuit will rapidly fill up with cold water. Likewise, if lies are not detected quickly, they will grow larger and lead us into a mental fog, where they can do even more damage. I call this process "falling into spiritual hypothermia."

1. Have you ever felt like you were in a fog, mentally or spiritually? Did you ever consider that the fog was the result of a spiritual attack? Why or why not?

2. Think of a situation where a lie of the enemy silently seeped into your thinking, putting you into a fog so that you felt confused, paralyzed, and unable to make a clear decision.

3.   Were you able to get out of that fog on your own, or did you need to reach out for help?

4.   If you reached out to someone else for help, how did processing the lies with them help you to get out of the fog?

5.   If you didn't reach out to someone else, what were you thinking that kept you from making that choice? (Pride, fear, worry, doubt, etc.?)

While watching news reports of the 2004 Indian Ocean tsunami, one thing that struck me was video footage of people standing on the beach and looking out to sea at the massive wave coming in the distance, yet they were unable to do anything. Many of them just stood there as if their feet were planted in the ground. Many survivors' stories recounted how they couldn't even remember how to swim until they heard someone call their name or grabbed hold of their hand.

Being able to see the lies coming, using your "God tools" to renew your mind, and reaching out to someone safe who understands both you and God's Word is your way of swimming. Not only will it keep you afloat, but it will guide you to safety when the waters get rough and high.

In our last small group session, we used four steps to untangle the lies we were drowning in. Just as with swimming lessons, one session isn't going to save your life when cold, rushing waters take your breath away and sweep you off your feet. The same is true in learning how to renew our minds. It's vital that we repeat what we've learned so that when difficult circumstances attempt to confuse us or knock us down, we are able to instinctively use our God tools for surviving those attacks.

6. Now that you've tracked your transformation over the past week, did you see improvement? If not, did you renew you mind with the truth whenever the lies began to seep back into your thinking?

At the beginning of this small group study, you were given instructions on how to fly solo, with a copilot, or with a crew. As you venture deeper *Into the Wilds*, I have no doubt that you'll discover more attempts by the enemy to take you out. When that happens, it means that you're getting too close to a truth that will set you free. The enemy hates that. Military pilots will tell you that defensive flak from the enemy is always the strongest when you're over the target. You will find that when you actively begin fighting against the lies with God's truth, the enemy will come up with new lies to attack you with. Expect it. Count on it.

Once you become proficient in recognizing the lies, and going after them with God's truth, you become a dangerous man—dangerous because you can now help other men untangle their own lies by teaching them to do what you've learned. That's called *discipleship*. It's what we're called to do. The enemy wants to back you down, take you out, and cause you to be afraid. The only way this happens is when you forget who you really are, your true identity—Christ in you! The enemy wants to put you back into a fog, where you can't clearly see who you are. Even when you think you are safe, he will sneak in through a back door you didn't even know existed.

> *Be clear-minded and alert. Your opponent, the Devil, is prowling around like a roaring lion, looking for someone to devour.*
>
> (1 Peter 5:8 isv)

The only way that we can be *"clear-minded"* is to continually renew our minds with God's truth. Look at Romans 12:2 again:

> *Do not conform to the pattern of this world, but be transformed by the renewing of your mind. Then you will be able to test and approve what God's will is—his good, pleasing and perfect will.*

As you repeat the Four Steps this week, be ruthless in the pursuit of God's truth by taking up the shield of faith and holding up God's Word against the lies of the enemy, so that you discover what God's will is—His good, pleasing and perfect will. Remember, if what you are believing is truth, you will experience the fruits of the Spirit found in Galatians 5:22–23:

> *But the fruit of the Spirit is love, joy, peace, forbearance, kindness, goodness, faithfulness, gentleness and self-control.*

THE FOUR STEPS

(Complete the following exercise)

1.   Identify any unhealthy emotions and write them down.

2.   Identify any unhealthy thoughts and write them down.

3.   Identify the truth and write it down.

4.   Renew your mind.

TRACK YOUR TRANSFORMATION

Write down the original thought, and the percentage you believed it to be true.

Example: Day 1—My wife left me, and without a woman, I'm a worthless loser.

Belief percentage = 100%

Write down the original thought again and what percentage you now believe it to be true.

Example: Day 3—My wife left me, and without a woman, I'm a worthless loser.

Belief percentage = 50%

Write down the original thought again and what percentage you now believe it to be true.

Example: Day 7—My wife left me, and without a woman, I'm a worthless loser.

Belief percentage = 0%

Remember: If you do not renew your mind with the truth, nothing changes!

In the same way a man becomes a better fisherman by learning to keep his lines from becoming tangled, the man who learns to untangle the lies in his own mind becomes a better fisher of men. There's a bond between men who fish together, hunt together, play sports together, go to war together, and pray together. Spend time praying together with the men of your group. Pray that God will give each man the strength and clarity they need when the fog gets thick and the flak becomes more intense as they learn to draw from God's strength and not their own. Encourage each other to keep going deeper *Into the Wilds*...together.

THE HOME FRONT

THE BIG FIVE AT HOME

Remember when I told you that the Big Five in Africa was a place where I had to face my emotions? Well, facing the terrifying things that crawl and slither across the floors of Africa was tough, but facing my wife when I don't know the right thing to say can be scarier than any black mamba or savannah lion. Some days, I feel as if she's just waiting for an opportunity to pounce if she smells any weakness or insecurity in me. When I'm not thinking straight, my fear of "not being good enough" or "not having the perfect words to say" can create crippling emotions, like fear and anger, which can lead to "fight or flight"—neither of which are good options. I find myself either defending or blaming, or trying to please her just to diffuse the situation.

Simply put, men and women do *not* think alike—ever! We see life differently, and we respond to life situations differently. I said it a couple of chapters ago and I'll repeat it now: you have to learn to take your spiritual temperature and drink your Man Tea when the attacks come. And believe me, they will come. Understanding and managing the thoughts and emotions in your relationships will save you more strife than you can possibly imagine.

If you're like a lot of men, your cellphone is on your nightstand and before you get up in the morning, you either check the weather, news, sports, email, or social media. The morning I wrote this, I was reading posts on Facebook when I saw a post (by a woman) of a large muscled man, dressed in a tank top and sweat pants, doing chores around the house. Here's her post:

FACTS!! The #1 thing that turns a woman on is when a man helps a woman around the house. Let her come home and see that he washed the dishes, cooked dinner, dusted the rooms, took out the trash, vacuumed the house, did the laundry, and she won't have anything to do but her man!

As I scrolled up to her next post, it was from a site called Hot Moms Club. It was a picture of a tattooed woman holding a little boy in her arms, with this caption: "A woman has one boy she will never lose feelings for: her son."

My immediate emotional response was one of anger, and if I could have removed my fingers from my throat, I could have posted a responsive rant that would have read something like this:

Yup, and you'll say you'll never lose feelings for your man either... as long as he washes dishes; cooks dinner; dusts the house; takes out the trash; vacuums the house; does laundry; rubs your feet after a hard day; listens for hours as you talk about the kids and your girlfriends; shows affection; engages in deep, meaningful conversation until there are no more words left on the planet; plans the next five date nights; sits for hours at the mall while you try on clothes; never says anything that would make you feel fat, skinny, or average; never looks in another woman's direction; and doesn't spend any time at the gym getting those big muscles in the picture the woman just drooled over, because he was hot!

Instead, I let all that hypocrisy penetrate my cerebral cortex for a few moments, slowed my breathing, choked back my gag reflex, and I read this woman's post immediately above the "#1 FACTS" post. It was from a site called GirlfriendsInGod:

No temptation has overtaken you except what is common to mankind. And God is faithful; he will not let you be tempted beyond what you can bear. But when you are tempted, he will also provide a way out so that you can endure it. (1 Corinthians 10:13)

FINDING YOUR "GOOD ENOUGH"

There are those moments when we all need a good reality check. Unlike in the movie *Jerry McGuire*, statements like "you complete me" and "you had me at hello" are simply not true for *both* men and women. We've romanticized those lines, worked them into books and movies, locker room talk, and girlfriends' table talk, but they stem from a lie. What's the root cause? *Coveting.* Any time you give another person the power to make you feel great about yourself (i.e., "you complete me"), you've also given them the power to use a glance or side comment to make you feel horrible about yourself. Remember that your "good enough" comes from Christ in you, not from external sources.

Almost on a weekly basis, some guy will call me, text me, or email me, saying that he is extremely angry with his wife, thinking about separating from her, or wants a divorce. When I ask him why, he almost always responds with, "I can't take her constant disrespect anymore. No matter what I do, it's never enough!" Just like the woman getting her self-worth from how she looks, this man is attempting to fill the same void with his wife's respect.

After listening to the man's anger and empathizing with his feelings, I usually ask this question: "If you didn't need your wife's respect, would you need to hit the wall, get separated, or file for divorce?"

Most of the time the response is the same: "No, but how do I get to the place where I don't need her respect? Doesn't the Bible say that wives are to respect their husbands?"

Yes, and men are also to love their wives.

This is an extremely sensitive topic, and one that has caused more heartache and anger than probably any other, especially within the church, and neither side feels heard. If a woman's need to be listened to would be deemed as important as a man's need for sex, there would probably be a lot of naked conversations going on!

Recently I was sitting in a staff meeting at church when the book title *His Needs and Her Needs* came up. It was not pretty. Here's how the conversation went.

Using lists in the book, my friend Derek wrote out the top five needs of a woman on the board. As he wrote them down, I watched the room. The women crossed their arms and smiled while the men shook their heads, sighed, and waited for the boot to drop.

WOMEN'S "BIG FIVE" NEEDS

1. Affection

2. Conversation

3. Honesty

4. Financial Support

5. Family Commitment

In case you didn't notice, domestic support was not one of the "Big 5" needs the woman's post on Facebook claimed to be number one; affection was number one.

After writing the Big 5 on the board, Derek asked all the men in the room to rate each of the woman's needs by using a 1 to 10 scale—10 being the most important. Here were the responses:

HOW MEN SCORED THE IMPORTANCE OF WOMEN'S NEEDS USING A 10-POINT SCALE

1. Affection – 10

2. Conversation – 10

3. Honesty – 10

4. Financial Support – 10

5. Family Commitment – 10

There were no smart aleck responses from the men, more of a sense of shame that they felt they should do better in each area. The woman's responses affirmed how important each of the five were to them, and how it makes them feel secure and loved when the man provides each of the five needs.

Next, Derek wrote down the top five needs of the man from the book.

MAN'S "BIG FIVE" NEEDS

1. Sexual Fulfillment

2. Recreational Companionship

3. An Attractive Spouse

4. Domestic Support

5. Admiration

Before Derek wrote down the second of the man's top five needs, all of the women in the room began to mock and complain about need #1: Sexual Fulfillment.

"That's all men want, *sex*! That's all they think about! Men just need to find a bathroom to get their frustrations out, and quit expecting the woman to do his dirty work for him!"

The look on the men's faces was unanimous: "Whoa! Where did that come from?"

Derek wrote down #2: Recreational Companionship.

What were the women's responses? "All men want is for a woman to go and do whatever *he* wants to do!"

Next came #3: An Attractive Spouse.

The response: "We can't compete with the young things you're looking at on porn sites and TV commercials. If that's what you want, you can just go find yourself some eighteen-year-old to fulfill your fantasies! We're outta here!"

Next, #4: Domestic Support.

The response: "All men want is a woman to pick up after them. You can clean the dang house yourself!" (finger snap included).

Finally, #5: Admiration.

The response: "You just want women to worship the ground you walk on while we get nothing in return."

Here's how the women scored the men's Big 5 needs:

HOW WOMEN SCORED THE IMPORTANCE OF MEN'S NEEDS USING A 10-POINT SCALE

1. Sexual Fulfillment – 2

2. Recreational Companionship – 2

3. An Attractive Spouse – 1

4. Domestic Support – 2

5. Admiration – 10

The men were beside themselves. "Ladies," some said, "now you can see why men feel so disrespected!"

Derek used this illustration to open up more conversation. He said, "Imagine the wife saying, 'If only our husbands would talk to us more, it would make life so much easier.' Then the husband answers, 'I have no interest in being feminized, so I'm not going to talk anymore the rest of the way home.' But how would the women have reacted if her husband said, 'I'll listen to you, but you need to take your clothes off first!' She would have been outraged."

The room fell silent.

Believe it or not, these needs are not made up. There is biblical support for both men's and women's needs.

WOMEN'S NEED: LISTENING AND HONESTY

This you know, my beloved brethren. But everyone must be quick to hear, slow to speak and slow to anger. (James 1:19 NASB)

Lying lips are an abomination to the Lord, but those who deal faithfully are His delight. (Proverbs 12:22 NASB)

MAN'S NEED: SEX

The marriage bed must be a place of mutuality—the husband seeking to satisfy his wife, the wife seeking to satisfy her husband. Marriage is not a place to "stand up for your rights." (1 Corinthians 7:5 MSG)

Or, as another translation begins the same verse: *"Stop depriving one another"* (NASB).

As a loving hind and a graceful doe, let her breasts satisfy you at all times; be exhilarated always with her love.   (Proverbs 5:19 NASB)

So then, what's the tie breaker? I mean, isn't that how this gets resolved? Here's what else the Bible says about our needs:

GETTING NEEDS MET BY ANYONE OTHER THAN CHRIST

If anyone comes to Me, and does not hate his own father and mother and wife and children and brothers and sisters, yes, and even his own life, he cannot be My disciple.   (Luke 14:26 NASB)

Put to death therefore what is earthly in you: sexual immorality, impurity, passion, evil desire, and covetousness [wanting what we don't have], *which is idolatry.*   (Colossians 3:5 ESV)

Since Jesus went through everything you're going through and more, learn to think like him. Think of your sufferings as a weaning from that old sinful habit of always expecting to get your own way. Then you'll be able to live out your days free to pursue what God wants instead of being tyrannized by what you want.   (1 Peter 4:1–2 MSG)

LOVE MORE, NEED LESS

One of the greatest principles for having a healthy marriage or relationship is based on the following: watch what God does, and then you do the same, like children who learn proper behavior from good parents. God's chief job is to love you. Keep company with Him and learn a life of love. Observe how Christ loved us. His love was not cautious but extravagant. He didn't love in order to get something from us, but to give everything of Himself to us. Love others like that.

God's commands to us are to love Him and to love others as we love ourselves. The problems begin when we think we have to have another person's love and respect in order to be content with ourselves. As long as our worth and value are dependent upon what others think about us, we will always try to manipulate them to get our needs met.

When women call men "pigs" because of their desire for sex or an attractive spouse, they are simply trying to find their "good enough," but to men, it comes out sounding like manipulation by putting men down. If a woman's worth and value comes from where her true beauty resonates, Christ in her, she wouldn't need to put men down or post on social media about all the things men should be doing better in order to gain her respect. If a man is secure in his true identity, Christ in him, he wouldn't instantly feel disrespected when he fails to get what he desires from his wife. Neither of them derive their worth and value from what others think of them. It *must* come from God's Spirit in them, or else they will be tyrannized and remain on the hamster wheel of performance, working hard to get what they want and feel they deserve, for the rest of their lives.

Unfortunately, we don't often hear this truth preached in churches. Most of the sermons I've sat through on this topic have been filled with statements like, "If you'll just do all these things for your spouse, they're going to want to do them for you in return. It's your Christian duty!" What a crock! You don't love out of obligation (which will only leave you angry and resentful); you love out of your true being, Christ in you, which needs nothing in return!

Here's the hard truth: there is no guarantee your spouse is going to change. Plus, if you're doing all these things to get your spouse to give you what you want, is that love...or manipulation? Any time we start a sentence with, "How do I get my spouse to...," we've started down a dangerous path of manipulation that is only going to leave you frustrated, angry, and insecure, causing you to "get" rather than "give" in your relationships. We must learn how to *love more* and *need less*.

It's amazing how quickly relationships can change and heal once the principle of "love more, need less" is applied. Did Jesus need to take from others to find His "good enough"? Did He use manipulation or control to get His needs met? No. How did He do it? His "true being" was brimming over into true words and deeds, because He was living out of the core of who He really was. Once again, look at Luke 6:43–45:

You don't get wormy apples off a healthy tree, nor good apples off a dis-
eased tree. The health of the apple tells the health of the tree. You must
begin with your own life-giving lives. It's who you are, not what you say
and do, that counts. Your true being brims over into true words and
deeds.   (MSG)

We have that same power through Christ in us when we live out of
God's Spirit, who came into us the moment we truly believed. The *false me*
always requires control and manipulation to get my needs met. When I'm
living in the *false me*, I destroy trust, push others away, and draw attention
to myself. The *true me* requires nothing, as I'm 100 percent compete "in
Christ." When I'm living in the *true me*, I build trust, create deep relationships, and draw people to Jesus.

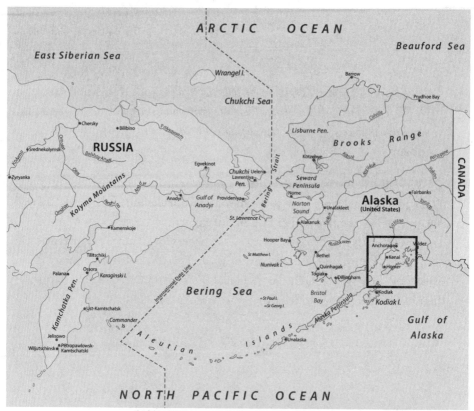

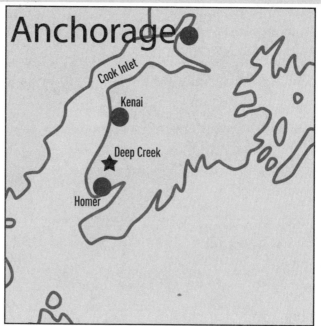

Cook Inlet and Deep Creek

THE WILDS

ZODIAC HEART ATTACK

My ears went completely silent, as if I'd sunk to the bottom of the deep end in a large swimming pool. The 9-mm pistol we were using to shoot halibut after getting them alongside the boat discharged less than two feet from my head, and missed puncturing the side of the inflatable Zodiac raft in which we were sitting by less than one inch! That might not have been that big a deal had we been fishing in July in the lower 48, but this happened about five miles out in Alaska's Cook Inlet, where the water temperature was cold enough to cause hypothermia in a matter of minutes, and certain death in about thirty minutes.

Just as my friend was about to pull the trigger to shoot the large halibut, an unexpected wave rocked our raft from behind. At the same time, the front of the Zodiac kicked toward the halibut, causing the firearm to discharge before my friend was ready. We looked at each other, both realizing at the same moment how close we'd just come to becoming the arctic waters' "deadliest catch!"

The day prior, we launched our 13-foot Zodiac with a 25-hp Yamaha motor into the pounding surf out of Deep Creek, Alaska. Other commercial fishing boats were being launched by huge alien-looking machines the logging industry calls "skidders." These boats were heading some twelve to fifteen miles out to sea to their favorite fishing spots. They were filled with groups of tourists paying two hundred fifty dollars each in hopes of catching a 100-pound halibut on rented poles so they could have the perfect photo opportunity taken while wearing designer fishing outfits that they would probably never wear again. Those treasured photos, however, will sit on their office desks for years to come, a reminder of how much they hate their jobs, and wish they were somewhere outside having the adventure of a lifetime.

We pushed the Zodiac into the surf, fired up the motor, angled the nose into the oncoming waves, and skipped the motorized raft toward the smoking volcano, some twenty-six miles across the frigid, rugged waters of Cook Inlet. We dropped anchor for the first time only three miles from shore. The tide was slack and the 16-ounce sinkers quickly found the bottom of the ocean in about sixty feet of water.

Posing with Alaska's giant halibut.

Within minutes, I landed my first halibut, and could only imagine what other huge fish awaited in the murky depths below. As we placed the catch on the stringer and began to bait our lines, the tide had been picking up speed with surprising force. As I bent over to get some squid bait out of the cooler, the anchor I thought was securely wedged on the ocean bottom suddenly and violently caught in a group of rocks. The jerking movement this caused thrust the nose of the boat down and into an oncoming eight-foot wave. Had this been an aluminum river boat, we would have been in the drink on the count of two, but the inflatable Zodiac, anchor rope stretched taut, pulled through the wave and bounced back up like a beach ball released from the bottom of a swimming pool. The next thing I saw were the black wooden floor boards of the Zodiac pressed against my nose, as the forceful wave had thrown me from one end of the boat to the other.

My first thought was, *Did a whale just grab our anchor line?*

I scrambled back to the front of the boat to try to untie the anchor rope, as we didn't have enough rope let out to keep the angle of the boat from pulling us down in the riptide. The tide was so strong, and the anchor so securely lodged, there was nothing I could do to get it to budge. As I pulled on the rope to move the raft forward, another wave hit us, pinning my hand between the nylon anchor rope and the nose of the boat. Had I not been wearing heavy rubber gloves, the skin on my hand certainly would have peeled off like hot wax. Somehow, the anchor let loose and we were able to let out more rope and return to fishing.

Within an hour, I hooked what I thought must have been a 200-pound halibut. I fought that fish on 130-pound test line for over thirty minutes! As I looked into the waters below the tip of my pole, I noticed something out of the corner of my eye. About three-quarters of a mile away, coming straight at us, was a massive cargo ship the size of a football field. Three-quarters of a mile may seem like a long way out, but when moving with Cook Inlet's powerful rip tides, that distance can be covered in about two minutes. I hadn't been able to bring the fish close enough to the boat to tell what it was, but we knew that it had better surface, and like right now, or that ship would be on us before we could pull up our anchor. By law, that commercial ship was required to give the right of way to our anchored boat. The problem was…it hadn't seen us.

About the time we were seriously contemplating cutting the fishing line, we noticed a dark, looming figure begin to emerge from beneath the boat. The moment the massive fish caught sight of our raft, it took off like a shot toward the bottom, and left the drag on my reel screaming like a stuck pig. Thinking the ship would surely change course, and also thinking we had a once-in-a-lifetime halibut on the line, we continued to fight the large fish.

Slowly, the intensity of the fight began to lessen, and I quickly began reeling it toward the Zodiac. When the huge fish was within seven feet of the surface, we realized that what we'd caught was not a huge halibut but instead a massive skate, a fish resembling a stingray, and not something we were interested in keeping.

Tired and frustrated, I began to raise my head to tell my friend it wasn't a halibut, but he wasn't looking at me or the fish, he was looking at the massive ship now only a hundred yards away and fast approaching. If we didn't move, we'd be crushed in a matter of seconds. My buddy feverishly began to pull in the anchor rope as I reached over the side to cut the line. It was going to be close. At the last second, the ship changed its course and veered to our left. The wake of the vessel threw our tiny raft around like a child's toy boat in a bathtub. All we could do was ride out the pounding waves, as trying to speed out of there would have resulted in dumping the raft.

After our close call, we decided we'd had enough adventure for one day, so we secured the anchor, our hooks and poles, fired up the outboard motor, and began heading back toward shore. As we approached the beach, I was never so happy to set my feet on dry land. We ended the day by cooking fresh halibut over a portable gas stove, along with some potatoes and onions in an open fire pit. There's no restaurant on earth I'd rather eat at than at Mother Nature's table.

The next morning, we made a quick run to the local Wal-Mart to pick up some more bait, a couple of 20-ounce sinkers, and a new "O" ring for our secondary gas can. The can had been leaking gasoline, and was now only about half full. One thing you can't chance is running out of gasoline miles into the inlet. You could be pulled out to sea by the tides, and that's pretty much a death sentence without a flare gun or an Emergency Position-Indicating Radio Beacon (EPIRB).

After filling our tank with six dollar-per-gallon gasoline, we headed back to camp, loaded up the Zodiac again, and launched this time into Deep Creek. Deep Creek is a great salmon stream, but it can go from being almost bone dry to over your head in only a couple of hours. I once heard a great story about a young guy from the lower 48, wanting to prove he could cross Deep Creek in his souped-up 4-wheel drive, who flooded his engine trying to cross a spot in the river that proved to be a little deeper than he thought. He got out, took his keys, and hitched a ride into town to find a tow-truck to pull him out. When the young man returned several hours later, the only thing he found was a buoy floating on the top of the water that a local fisherman had tied onto the vehicle so the owner would be able to find it when he returned. Like I've said, Alaska can eat your lunch in a heartbeat if you're not paying attention.

As we came out of the mouth of Deep Creek, the waves suddenly tripled in size, as the creek flowed across a delta for about a quarter-mile. Then, just as suddenly, it dropped off about sixty feet. Twenty-two years prior, in that very spot, my friend and his pregnant wife had put their lives on the line to rescue several fishermen whose boat had capsized in the bone-chilling waters. At the time, they were in a 17-foot Zodiac, which was four feet longer than the one we were in. That extra four feet gave them more stability on the huge waves, and helped them navigate the churning waters around the mouth of Deep Creek. We weren't too worried about the waves this day, as the waters were relatively calm, and there were halibut to be caught!

Catching a shark.

For the next four hours, we fished the downside of high tide until the tides went slack. We hadn't been catching much, so we decided to move out into the inlet a few more miles. After about thirty minutes of fishing in the new spot, my friend hooked what we thought was a monster. It ended up being another skate that was truly half the size of our boat. When they decide they don't want to be caught, they just open up their water wings and head for the bottom, and all you can do is hold on for the ride! I think the thing that's exciting about fishing ocean waters is that you never know what might grab ahold of your line.

About the time we got the skate off of the line, I noticed three commercial fishing boats headed into shore a couple hours ahead of schedule. If I'd have done the math, I might have figured out why they were headed in, but at the time, I was busy reeling in a five-foot sand shark. As the minutes turned into hours, the tides began to change, the winds picked up, and the current was going back out to sea...and so were we! Our anchor had come undone, and we were ripping along with the current.

On the other side of the inlet, dark, looming clouds began to wrap their arms around one of Alaska's giant volcanoes. On the horizon, entire mountain ranges were beginning to evaporate from sight. Realizing what was coming, we immediately pulled anchor and began to make the trek back to Deep Creek in hopes of hitting the mouth of the inlet before low tide, and avoiding the wrath on the oncoming storm.

We hadn't made it a mile when the small waves began to turn into rollers with the rushing winds. They reached so high that we couldn't see the shore every time we hit the trough of another wave. Some of the waves were so large the Zodiac literally fell off the top of the wave in a free fall, as coolers, fishing poles, spare gas cans, and halibut floated three feet in the air only to come crashing down again. This was no longer my idea of fun. In smooth waters, a Zodiac can get up on step and fly across the water like a rocket. We were barely idling, just trying to keep the boat from capsizing as we crawled toward the shore.

As we got within a half-mile of shore, we could see the 150-foot cliffs that surround the mouth of Deep Creek. This was going to be a real shot in the dark to try to find the creek's mouth and its safe haven. We were only going to get one shot at this because of the strong rip tide and the enormous waves that were now pounding one after another in rapid succession. With the combination of high winds and Alaska's drastic tidal changes, the approach to the mouth was going to be a doozy. If you have to turn around in that delta, there's a better than average chance you're going into the drink. Our tiny Zodiac was beginning to get thrashed and I was openly praying for God's help.

My friend shouted for me to let go of the rope I was desperately clinging on to and to make my way to the front of the boat once we hit the shallows. I needed to keep an eye out for low water, because if you run aground with this deadly surf, it is next to impossible to get things turned around and back into deep water without getting off the boat. If you have to get out to dislodge the boat, one wrong step and the current will pull you under and out to sea, or the next one hundred waves will pound you against the rocky bottom as you try to come up for air.

A tsunami of emotions washed over me as memories raced through my mind of working on the fishing boat in Bristol Bay and watching an Italian fishing boat sink beside us in 1985. I clearly remembered the looks of terror and panic on the crew's faces as they threw their gear onto a sister ship while also trying to put on their PDFs (personal floatation devices). I was already wearing my PDF, but being so far from shore and no one being able to reach us, the threat of hypothermia leading to drowning in nonstop waves of icy-cold seawater was becoming a real possibility.

Before I could grasp an oar to measure the water depth, our motor suddenly hit bottom, and the forward momentum of the boat came to a sudden and complete halt! Before we knew what was happening, the first of many waves began crashing over the boat, sending our gear flying through the air. What we were doing wasn't working. We needed to do something different...right now!

We had a couple of choices, but the only choice that didn't include us dying in the storyline involved us jumping from the boat, still a quarter-mile from shore, in order to get it turned around and headed back out to sea. Human instinct sees the shore ahead of you and tempts you to push forward toward the beach. Had we done that, we would have died, no question. The choice we had to make was to turn the boat around and push the nose directly into the oncoming waves so we could go with the current back into the mouth of the storm. Horrifying, but survivable.

With the waves crashing on top of us, we finally got the boat turned around and pointed back out to sea. With every wave we hit, the front of the boat pointed straight up into the air at a 45-degree angle, before plummeting to the bottom of the next trough, until we got out of harm's way.

Thirty minutes later, we ditched the raft about a half-mile up the shoreline, but at a spot where we were able to get out of the boat without the fear of drowning. As we climbed out, the water inside the boat was almost flush to the top, and yet it still floated! No other type of boat could have survived our predicament, and any other decision we could have made to get out of our circumstance prematurely would have led to certain death.

That night, as I lay in my sleeping bag listening to the rain and the wind pound our tent, I was never so thankful to be back on dry land. I kept thinking about our week, and the trials we'd faced, and the Holy Spirit brought a verse to mind:

Consider it a sheer gift, friends, when tests and challenges come at you from all sides. You know that under pressure, your faith-life is forced into the open and shows its true colors. So don't try to get out of anything prematurely. Let it do its work so that you become mature and well-developed, not deficient in any way. If you don't know what you're doing, pray to the Father. He loves to help. You'll get his help, and won't be condescended to when you ask for it. Ask boldly, believing, without a second thought. People who "worry their prayers" are like wind-whipped waves. Don't think you're going to get anything from the Master that way, adrift at sea, keeping all your options open.

(James 1:2–8 MSG)

Our challenges on the Zodiac were difficult, but they are nothing compared to the challenges that I've faced in my life in the real world. I've had to deal with my emotions. I've had to learn to spot and evade the arrows, to be discipled, and to trust that God has a plan for me. And so must you! The flaming arrows are there to deceive you, and the challenges you will face out there are not easy, because the world isn't easy. God didn't intend for us to have to live our lives on the edge, awaiting our next battle while we ride out the next storm, and the enemy refuses to lay down his weapons. But God has given you the weapons you need to do battle…and to win in *this* life.

Jesus conquered sin and death, but you have to be trained in how to use that power. You *will* face challenges, there *will* be storms, and waves *will* smack you hard, dead in the face. So you *must* learn to fight back using the most powerful weapon God's made available to you in your arsenal. "Christ in you" is the source of your strength.

Anyone who meets a testing challenge head-on and manages to stick it out is mighty fortunate. For such persons loyally in love with God, the reward is life and more life. (James 1:12 MSG)

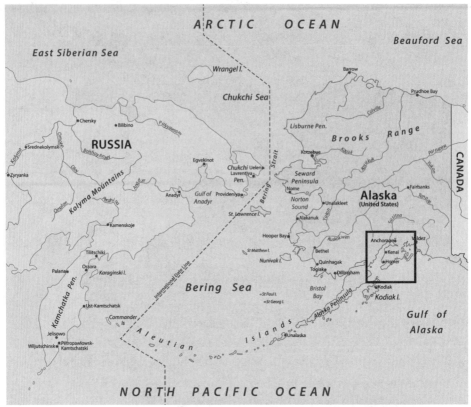

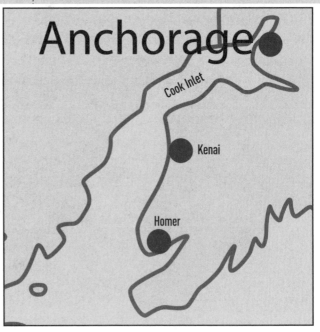

Cook Inlet

7

GETTING OUT OF
THE STORM

Things do not change; we change.
—*Henry David Thoreau*

I
f you're planning on adventuring in Alaska, or other crazy places, you
need to realize that, until Jesus comes back, there are still going to be
incredible dangers. You might be called upon to reach deep within yourself
and let go of your control. You may be challenged to risk your own safety
in order to take the next step. Volcanoes will erupt, earthquakes are going to happen, tsunamis and storms rage on—those things aren't going to
change. However, tides do change, and you'd better know how to handle
them when they do.

TURNAGAIN ARM

Cook Inlet was named for none other than legendary explorer Captain
James Cook, who happened along this way while looking for the Northwest
Passage in 1778. While searching for the elusive passage, something that
never existed to begin with, some of Cook's crew were nearly swamped
and drowned by the extreme tidal change in an offshoot of the inlet. Cook
named this place Turnagain Arm, in honor of the extreme tides there,
which come in like a breaking wave.

The tidal change in Turnagain Arm is thirty-five feet. When you combine that tidal change with the "primary oscillation" of Turnagain Arm,
the natural sloshing back and forth of the water in the basin, the result is
a tide that comes in as a single wave, called a "tidal bore." The bore tide is

a huge wave, or series of waves, that advance down Turnagain Arm in a wall of water up to ten feet high. It's a dramatic show of nature's power. Cook Inlet has the second largest tides in North America, slightly less than Canada's Bay of Fundy, which has the highest tidal range in the world.

Tourists line the shores south of Anchorage to watch Turnagain Arm's dramatic tidal bore. There are numerous signs warning people not to get too close to the water. If people would just read and pay attention to these signs, they'd stay out of trouble. But every year, emergency calls for help go out for people who ignore the warnings, get stuck in the soft mud flats, and drown.

After repeated expeditions, Captain Cook realized these tides weren't going to change, nor would the fresh water in the tides ever turn into the salt water that he hoped would lead him to a Northwest Passage. Eventually, he was forced to turn around and find a better way. He had to change.

Many of us battle the tide of our thoughts and emotions day by day, sometimes minute by minute. Our lives seem to mirror the tides. One moment, we're filling up, riding high on a wave, but before long, it feels like the bottom is being sucked out from under us, and we're being pulled out to sea. Why is that?

CHANGING THE WAY YOU THINK

This is all part of Satan's plan. He wants Christians to be wishy-washy about their faith, about their righteousness. He doesn't want you to know that your righteousness is secure, and that God is a safe Anchorage. (Anchorage means "a source of security, something that supplies a secure hold for something else.") Satan doesn't want you to know that you can survive the toughest storms.

So how do we go about believing that we are righteous? And an equally big question: how does my behavior undergo transformation?

All around us, we see Christian friends falling apart: husbands committing adultery; moms taking multiple medications trying to find their way out of depression; men exploding after years of bottling up their anger; young men enslaved by porn and lust; struggling pastors rejected and abandoned by their churches; and families in financial distress. I'm sure you can add to the list.

And yet, each week, we go to church dressed in our Sunday best. We pray. We read our Bibles. We reluctantly take our turn serving in the nursery. We give our ten percent. We toss and turn at night, panicked by anxiety, angry at our spouse, overwhelmed with our teenager's choices—and with no relief in sight. Some of us pile into buses filled with other men and attend massive Christian stadium events in hopes that, somehow, something will be different this time. We work all day, then wake up and do it all over again. We try to do our best, but our Bible reading, church-going, and personal efforts just don't seem to be enough to bring about change.

Jesus said,

If you just use my words in Bible studies and don't work them into your life, you are like a dumb carpenter who built a house but skipped the foundation. When the swollen river came crashing in, it collapsed like a house of cards. It was a total loss.   (Luke 6:48–49 MSG)

You can feel the bore tide of thoughts and emotions overtaking you, but you don't know how to get out of the way or get it together before all is lost. It's like you're trying to run in a new direction, but the circular path is the one you keep choosing.

It's like we're insane. A statement often misattributed to Albert Einstein defines insanity this way: Doing the same thing over and over again and expecting different results.

So how do our lives become transformed?

The answer is simple, but it's not easy: you have to change the way you think.

God's part is the gift of righteousness. Your part is changing the way you think. Or, to put it another way, let God transform you into a new person by changing the way you think.

Here are the words of Paul in Romans12:2:

And do not be conformed to this world, but be transformed by the renewing of your mind, so that you may prove what the will of God is, that which is good and acceptable and perfect.   (NASB)

Until we put the polluted thoughts in our brain through the filter of God's truth, we're going to continue to live messed-up lives.

STRONG, LIKE A CLAM

This filter is not much different than the way a clam uses seawater to siphon away the sand so that it can dig deep to escape predators. I've spent many hours digging for razor clams in Cook Inlet, Alaska. They are sleek, beautiful, and well-fortified. An adult razor clam's shell is a dark, glossy olive green and brown. The interior is white to purplish-brown. If a clam feels threatened, it extends its foot (an apparatus that resembles a tongue) and forces blood into it. The foot enlarges and literally anchors the clam in place, making it difficult for even the biggest of men to pull it out of the sand. These clams can grow up to eleven inches in length and live to be fifteen years old.

Inside, razor clams have a pair of siphons they use for filtering water, food, and sand. These long siphons extrude out the side of the shell from the clam's mantle, and reach up to the water above. Water and food particles are drawn in through one siphon and into the gills, where tiny, hair-like cilia move the water, and food is caught in mucus on the gills. Here, the gills draw oxygen from the water flow, and this mixture of food and water is then transported to the clam's mouth, where it can digest the nutrients. A second siphon carries away the remaining water, filtering out the sand.

Prying these well-fortified shells open is not an easy task. An elastic ligament connects the two shell layers. The only way to open the outer shell is to submerge the clam in boiling water. The extreme high temperatures cause the razor clam to die, which releases the ligament that's been holding the outer shell closed.

When I first tried digging Cook Inlet razor clams, I was horrible at it. I would bring up about one clam for every ten I lost. Before long, I was cold and tired, my hands were sliced up, and I was feeling pretty deflated. But in time, and with the help of a friend who had much more experience in digging up clams than I did, I began to be able to dig deeper and faster than the clams. His support and guidance kept me from quitting in frustration.

Digging for truth to renew our minds is a similar process. Most men don't know where to go to find truth to replace the lies the enemy is shooting through their brains. When we have someone who knows where to dig deep and find truth, who knows how to filter out the lies, then we can escape the grip of the enemy.

But, even though someone may be able to help you locate Scripture to debunk the lies Satan is throwing at you, until God's truth has been revealed to you, nothing in your life will change. You can't make it happen through your own hard effort. It's those "hitting bottom" moments that break our outer shell (our flesh and mind), and cause transformational beliefs to occur at our core. These truths can only come from the Father. These are God's "aha!" moments.

Even though you may be able to dig up Cook Inlet razor clams on a consistent basis, you still have to get through that outer shell to get to the good stuff on the inside. What breaks a razor clam's grip? Dropping them into boiling water heated by a raging fire. What causes my outer self to break? What allows me to shed the false belief that I need the good opinion of others or that I need to perform for my worth? Being exposed to the fire. Not a fire imposed by other people through their controlling and manipulating shame and guilt, but by the fire of God's truth that burns off Satan's lies. As a believer, I am His child, and I am 100 percent righteous "in Christ!"

God will allow us to journey into dangerous waters and even have personal shipwrecks so that, eventually, we will come to that place where we are broken under the weight of our sin, where we can finally hear the voice of truth and find true freedom!

INTO THE WILDS FIELD GUIDE

CHAPTER SEVEN: GETTING OUT OF THE STORM

Some men love adventure, the hairier the better. Other men, however, love adventure as long as it is safe, predictable, and manageable. They wear the latest gear, put on the hat and T-shirt, and try to look the part, but if it means risking actually going into the wilds, many men will make excuses and look for a way out. They'd rather drive than fly, walk than run, and crawl than jump. They've embraced their fears and learned to blindly rely on their GPS, rather than venturing where the winding road takes them. Some will only jump as long as there's a safety net and the drop isn't too far. Others will jump as long as people are watching, or as long as they receive kudos from the crowd. But, what happens when that man's left to his own devices?

When the sun goes down and the clouds roll in, shadows and strange sounds can take on the appearance of something evil lurking in the night. The encroaching darkness and the echoing sounds mean that a man can no longer depend upon his eyes and ears. When freezing night rain numbs his senses, and hypothermia begins to set in without a fire to warm up his core, panic and confusion can overwhelm and a man can no longer depend upon his sense of touch or trust his thoughts. If that man is alone or doesn't get out of there quickly…he's dead.

What authentic wilderness men understand is this: **you never, ever, go into the wilds alone.**

Yet, men keep going back to the same place, alone, expecting different results. Here's an often-used definition of insanity: *Doing the same thing over and over again and expecting different results.*

This week's study isn't going to be easy. I'm going to ask you to risk doing something different—something much harder than anything you've done so far. I'm going to ask you to not keep going back to that "thing" in which you're attempting to find your "good enough." This week, I'm going to ask you to identify the things that are causing you to stay stuck in the storm, and to do this, you may have to make the journey back into the storm to find your way out (just as I had to do at Cook Inlet in the section, Zodiac Heart Attack).

It's important to remember that God cares more about what's causing you to sin than the sin itself. He knows your story and understands why your thoughts are unhealthy, but He doesn't justify your story as a reason to stay in your sin or unhealthiness. He wants you to be free! The focus of this exercise isn't on any specific sin you're struggling with (i.e., porn, affairs, money, title, performance, etc.). Those actions/sins are merely the unhealthy fruit hanging on the tree. The goal is to get at the root cause of the storm itself. In order to get out of the storm, you have to *want* to be rescued.

1. Make a list of the things you struggle with that are destroying your thought life. (Example: Because I believe I have to have my wife's respect, it's causing me to lash out at her when I feel she's being disrespectful.) Remember, if you don't feel that it is safe to share this with some of the men in your group, I encourage you to find someone safe you can share with.

2. What are the underlying beliefs beneath the thoughts that are keeping you stuck? (Example: **Thought**—*If my coworker would sleep with me, I'd feel more like a man.* **Belief**—*My worth and value comes from what my coworker thinks of me.*)

The reason sin is so attractive is because it almost always delivers an immediate payoff. The reason we stay stuck in our sins, or unhealthy behaviors, is because we're getting something out of them.

3. What do you see as the benefits you're getting from your unhealthy behaviors?

4. What are the possible costs to you, or those you love, by choosing to continue the unhealthy behaviors?

5. If you didn't need whatever it is that's causing you to act out, how different would your life be? What might that look like?

It's time to light a fire beneath the core lie that's keeping us caught in the storm:

COVETING

Definition of *covet* from *Merriam-Webster's Dictionary*: 1.) to wish for earnestly: *covet* an award; 2.) to desire (what belongs to another) inordinately or culpably: The king's brother *coveted* the throne.

Whenever we wish for or desire what we don't have, we give that thing or person power over us, and by doing so, we are choosing to remain stuck in the storm. In reality, what we are believing is that we are not "complete" without it, or them. We've created idols out of those things or people, and thus, we give them more power over us than Christ in us!

Read the following verses aloud, then read the same verse in first person.

> *Since Jesus went through everything you're going through and more, learn to think like him. Think of your sufferings as a weaning from that old sinful habit of always expecting to get your own way. Then you'll be able to live out your days free to pursue what God wants instead of being tyrannized by what you want.* (1 Peter 4:1–2 MSG)

Let's restate that in the first person:

Since Jesus went through everything I'm going through and more, I'm learning to think like Him. I think of my sufferings as a weaning from that old sinful habit of always expecting to get my way. Then I'm able to live out my days free to pursue what God wants instead of being tyrannized by what I want.

6.   Did reading the verse in first person make it feel any different to you? How so?

Read the following verse aloud, then read the same verse in first person.

No one can serve two masters. Either you will hate the one and love the other, or you will be devoted to the one and despise the other. You cannot serve both God and money.   (Matthew 6:24)

The same verse in the first person:

I can't serve two masters. Either I will hate the one and love the other, or I will be devoted to the one and despise the other. I cannot serve both God and money.

7.   Where in my life are these verses connecting right now?

8.   What revelation is the Holy Spirit showing me through these verses?

When hunting on safari, it's necessary to leave the safety of your all-terrain vehicle and walk into the waist-high grass. Experienced safari guides with high-powered rifles will lead the way, as lions and leopards almost always attack from the front.

9.   If you're like most men, this is what it feels like when being asked to open up in a group setting. Are you finding it's getting easier to open up? If so, why?

10. By now, you're getting to know the men on a more personal level. How has that helped you in your process of getting out of the storms the enemy has been pounding you with?

It's not easy to break free from the things that control us. But if we truly want to get out of the storm, we sometimes have to be willing to journey back into the storm in order to find our way out. And, once again, remember our credo: Never, ever, go into the storm alone...which means you don't come out alone either. And when you do, you come out stronger and closer than ever before. In the wild, men have each other's backs. The journey will be hard, but because Christ is in you, you have what it takes to make the trip.

THE HOME FRONT

BILL'S FOUR STEPS

When Bill stepped through the double wooden doors, it was as if all the holiday cheer was sucked out of the room. His clothes were hanging on him from the loss of weight, and his cheeks were starting to sink in. The circles under his eyes hung down like Christmas wreaths, and he had a thousand-yard stare like that of soldiers who return from the battlefront.

A waitress brought us glasses of tea and said she'd be back to take our orders. I started the conversation.

"Boy, it's really cold outside, isn't it? I was afraid I was going to get stuck on the way here. So tell me, what have you been up to?"

It was as if time stood still as I waited for his response. He was having trouble speaking.

"Brent," he finally stammered, "I don't know if you know my story or not, but about five years ago, I had an affair. The church released me from my duties as senior pastor, and my wife and I separated. We're working on our marriage but it's been really hard. She keeps bringing up my past. Whenever I see someone from the church, they usually turn away like they don't see me, or they come over to me and say the typical comment: 'We've been praying for you.' I don't think I can take much more of this. Most of the time, I wish I'd never been born."

Bill went on.

"You know, the funny thing is that I still really care about those people. You just don't stop loving the ones you've served, and those you've given a huge piece of your life to."

In many ways, I could relate to what Bill was going through.

"How can I help?" I asked.

"Brent, I still feel like I'm called to ministry, but I know there's no way that could happen."

"Why is that?"

"Well, what would others think of me if I went back into the ministry?"

"Why do you care so much about what others think?"

"I don't know," he admitted. "I've been trying so hard to do the right things to prove I'm still a good man. Even after going through counseling for several years now, I still feel so unworthy."

"Unworthy to God or others?"

"Both, I guess."

I repeated what I'd heard Bill say to me. I let him know that I was hurting for him and that he wasn't alone in this. I reached into my computer bag, pulled out a pen and a tablet of paper, and handed it to Bill.

"Bill, I can relate to your story more than you know. I'd like you to do an exercise with me. It's what we call 'the Four Steps.' This is something another Christian man shared with me that has helped me weather some pretty powerful storms. I want you to write the words 'Identify the Unhealthy Emotions' on the top line. Then, beneath it, I'd like you to write out the unhealthy emotions you've experienced most regarding your affair."

STEP ONE: IDENTIFY UNHEALTHY EMOTIONS

Bill wrote:

Identify the Unhealthy Emotions:

Shame

Condemnation

"Great!" I said. "Now I'd like to ask you what percentage, on a scale of one to one hundred, you'd say you've been experiencing shame around your sin."

"Honestly, Brent, I'd say I'm experiencing shame and condemnation 100 percent."

"Okay, Bill, then write down 100 percent beside those emotions."

He did so.

"Bill," I asked, "from all your years of studying God's Word, do you really think He wants you to experience shame and condemnation?"

"No. I know he doesn't. But then, why am I?"

"We'll get to that, Bill, but the second thing I want you to do is write down the words 'Identify the Unhealthy Thoughts,' and beneath it, jot down the unhealthy thoughts that cause you to feel shame."

STEP TWO: IDENTIFY UNHEALTHY THOUGHTS

Bill wrote again:

Identify the Unhealthy Thoughts:

What are others thinking of me?

Is God punishing me for my sin?

Next, I had Bill take out his Bible, turn to 2 Corinthians 10:5–6, and read it out loud.

We demolish arguments and every pretension that sets itself up against the knowledge of God, and we take captive every thought to make it obedient to Christ. And we will be ready to punish every act of disobedience, once your obedience is complete.

Bill looked up at me and asked, "Doesn't that mean God is punishing me for my disobedience?"

"Here's my translation," I said. "We use our powerful God-tools for smashing warped philosophies, tearing down barriers erected against the truth of God, fitting every loose thought, emotion, and impulse into the structure of life shaped by Christ. Our tools are already at hand for clearing the ground of every obstruction and building lives of obedience into maturity."

"Brent, that sounds so different."

"Bill, God doesn't want to punish you or 'get you' for your sin. So many Christians confuse God's discipline with punishment. God's discipline is not punishment. Discipline is about helping to shape our actions in the future, training us to become more like Christ. Punishment is connected to what we've done in our past, and Jesus already hung on the cross for that."

"I know—it's just so hard to believe that sometimes, and my doubt leaves me feeling unworthy and depressed."

"Bill, God is a loving Father who's more concerned with growing you up, not tearing you down. He is not the one authoring your feelings of unworthiness or causing your depression."

I handed him my copy of *The Message* and had him read Hebrews 12:4–11:

In this all-out match against sin, others have suffered far worse than you, to say nothing of what Jesus went through—all that bloodshed! So don't feel sorry for yourselves. Or have you forgotten how good parents treat children, and that God regards you as his children?

My dear child, don't shrug off God's discipline, but don't be crushed by it either. It's the child he loves that he disciplines; the child he embraces, he also corrects.

God is educating you; that's why you must never drop out. He's treating you as dear children. This trouble you're in isn't punishment; it's training, the normal experience of children. Only irresponsible parents leave children to fend for themselves. Would you prefer an irresponsible God? We respect our own parents for training and not spoiling us, so why not embrace God's training so we can truly live? While we were children, our parents did what seemed best to them. But God is doing what is best for us, training us to live God's holy best. At the time, discipline isn't much fun. It always feels like it's going against the grain. Later, of course, it pays off handsomely, for it's the well-trained who find themselves mature in their relationship with God.

"Bill," I asked, "whose opinion is the only one that matters?"

"God's."

"Exactly! *Jesus* died for your sins, not other people. His is the only opinion that matters. You can't earn more of God's forgiveness. His forgiveness was made complete on the cross. You no longer have to be held hostage by others' opinions."

"Amen to that," the waitress said as she stepped up to the table. "I've been working on that one myself! Are you gentlemen ready to order yet?"

"No, sorry. Can you give us a few more minutes?" I smiled.

"Sure thing, honey! Take your time. Our special today is the blackened trout, and it's amazing!"

"Brent, can you show me where in the Bible it says I'm free of others' opinions?"

"Absolutely! Here are two verses that nail that coffin shut."

I first read Galatians 6:14:

For my part, I am going to boast about nothing but the Cross of our Master, Jesus Christ. Because of that Cross, I have been crucified in relation to the world, set free from the stifling atmosphere of pleasing others and fitting into the little patterns that they dictate.　　(MSG)

Then I read from Galatians 2:19–20:

What actually took place is this: I tried keeping rules and working my head off to please God, and it didn't work. So I quit being a "law man" so that I could be God's man. Christ's life showed me how, and enabled me to do it. I identified myself completely with him. Indeed, I have been crucified with Christ. My ego is no longer central. It is no longer important that I appear righteous before you or have your good opinion, and I am no longer driven to impress God. Christ lives in me. The life you see me living is not "mine," but it is lived by faith in the Son of God, who loved me and gave himself for me. I am not going to go back on that.　　(MSG)

"Bill, is it not clear to you that to go back to that old rule-keeping, peer-pleasing religion would be an abandonment of everything personal and free in my relationship with God? I refuse to do that, to repudiate God's grace. If a living relationship with God could come by rule-keeping, then Christ died unnecessarily."

"Brent, why have I never heard those verses that way before?"

"It's probably because they weren't revealed to you yet. You were so caught up in a performance lie that you couldn't hear them. Your hitting bottom has transformed your spiritual eyes to be able to see things you never saw before. Bill, now I want you to write down the words 'Identify the Truth' and let's identify a few verses about what God says about condemnation since that was one of your unhealthy emotions, and then write them down!"

STEP THREE: IDENTIFY THE TRUTH

Once again, Bill put pen to paper:

Identify the Truth:

Therefore, there is now no condemnation for those who are in Christ Jesus, because through Christ Jesus the law of the Spirit who gives life has set you free from the law of sin and death. (Romans 8:1–2)

For God did not send his Son into the world to condemn the world, but to save the world through him. (John 3:17)

"Great!" I said. "Now, what does God say about your sin? As a believer, is there anything you can do to separate yourself from the love of God? Is God keeping a record of specific sins so that you should be afraid of Him and unsure of your salvation?"

Bill started flipping pages and adding to his list of God's Truths.

Identify the Truth:

No, in all these things we are more than conquerors through him who loved us. For I am convinced that neither death nor life, neither angels nor demons, neither the present nor the future, nor any powers, neither height nor depth, nor anything else in all creation, will be able to sepa-

rate us from the love of God that is in Christ Jesus our Lord.

(Romans 8:37–39)

…as far as the east is from the west, so far has he removed our trans-gressions from us.   (Psalm 103:12)

"Bill, did God only conquer 'certain sins,' or did His sacrifice cover all sin?"

Bill's fingers began flipping pages once again, and he began adding to his list.

Identify the Truth:

*God went for the jugular when he sent his own Son. He didn't deal with the problem as something remote and unimportant. In his Son, Jesus, he personally took on the human condition, entered the disordered mess of struggling humanity in order to set it right **once and for all**.*

(Romans 8:3–4 MSG)

If we walk in the Light as He Himself is in the Light, we have fellow-ship with one another, and the blood of Jesus His Son cleanses us from all sin. If we say that we have no sin, we are deceiving ourselves and the truth is not in us. If we confess our sins, He is faithful and righteous to forgive us our sins and to cleanse us from all unrighteousness.

(1 John 1:7–9 NASB)

"I know these verses, Brent, but I haven't looked at them in quite a while. The storm of emotions I experience anytime I think of moving back into ministry paralyzes me with fear. I feel stuck and I'm not making any movement. Why is that?"

"Frankly, Bill, it's because you have to work them into your life. Remember, this is called 'the Four Step.' This is where step four comes into play."

STEP FOUR: RENEW YOUR MIND

"Romans 12:2 tells us to '*be transformed by the renewing of your mind*' so that we will be able to test and approve what God's will is—his good, pleasing and perfect will. It's not enough to just write down the unhealthy emotions, unhealthy thoughts, and scriptural truth; you also have to renew your mind with that truth. Keep writing down God's truths, read them aloud to yourself, have others read them to you, put them on your mirror, heck...stick them on your forehead if you need to. Whatever it takes so that you can filter Satan's lies through God's truth in order to break your unhealthy thought patterns, and transform you into the man God created you to be. But it's not just reading His truth that changes us—it's also by dwelling on that truth and working it into our lives!"

The waitress returned. "Well, gentlemen, have you decided what you're having for lunch today?"

"I think that fresh trout sounds incredible," said Bill.

"I'll have that as well," I replied.

For the next ten minutes, I shared with Bill the story of my own personal shipwreck, and how hitting bottom had changed my life.

"Bill," I said at the end of my story, "I wouldn't change what I went through for anything in the world."

The waitress placed two porcelain plates in front of us, covered with brown rice, vegetables, and fresh trout. She then refilled our glasses, and moved on to another table.

The first bite of trout made us sit back in our chairs and sigh with delight.

"So you're telling me," Bill went on, "that this 'hitting bottom' experience I'm going through is a good thing? That's kind of hard to swallow, but this fish on the other hand...."

"Bill, in Alaska, one of my favorite things to do after catching fresh halibut is to cook it right there on the shore, along with some potatoes and onions. We build a fire using cottonwood and coal, baste fish with some hot, sizzling butter, season it, then place the dusted filet in the pan and place it over an open flame. But what is it exactly that cooks the fish? Is it the wood? What about the pan? Maybe it's the butter, or the seasoning? What is it that takes this raw piece of fish, and transforms it into something that tastes so good?"

Without hesitation, Bill responded, "It's the flame. Brent, I've had so many sleepless nights around all of this. But now I feel so free after going through God's truths and promises!"

"Bill, when we started this conversation, you said you were experiencing shame and condemnation 100 percent. I'm curious, what percentage would you say you're experiencing that now?"

Bill took his list, wrote down a number at the bottom of the page, and then turned it so I could see it.

Shame and Condemnation: 10%

His response tells the story.

What a huge transformation in a little over an hour! What changed? Bill's thoughts changed.

What changed them? He was transformed by the renewing of his mind. His belief system was now in line with what God says, and he truly believed that his sins had been forgiven—*and* forgotten! Bill was so excited, he couldn't wait to "get back into the game!" He'd been given his life back. Bill was free. Free to live a life "in Christ!"

There was silence. I looked at Bill's face, and his eyes had welled up with tears. "He had to allow me to get to the end of my rope, didn't he?"

Bill opened his Bible and turned to Matthew 5:3–5:

You're blessed when you're at the end of your rope. With less of you there is more of God and his rule. You're blessed when you feel you've lost what is most dear to you. Only then can you be embraced by the One most dear to you. You're blessed when you're content with just who you are—no more, no less. That's the moment you find yourselves proud owners of everything that can't be bought. (MSG)

Bill turned to one last passage from 2 Corinthians 12:7–10:

Because of the extravagance of those revelations, and so I wouldn't get a big head, I was given the gift of a handicap to keep me in constant touch with my limitations. Satan's angel did his best to get me down; what he in fact did was push me to my knees. No danger then of walk-

ing around high and mighty! At first I didn't think of it as a gift, and begged God to remove it. Three times I did that, and then he told me,

My grace is enough; it's all you need. My strength comes into its own in your weakness.

Once I heard that, I was glad to let it happen. I quit focusing on the handicap and began appreciating the gift. It was a case of Christ's strength moving in on my weakness. Now I take limitations in stride, and with good cheer, these limitations that cut me down to size—abuse, accidents, opposition, bad breaks. I just let Christ take over! And so the weaker I get, the stronger I become. (MSG)

You see, everything we've talked about in this chapter is a challenge that could present itself in your life, and what we've discovered is that *challenges are gifts*, as they bring us closer to the truth and cause us to trust in God.

When you are challenged by the opinions of others, you need to renew your mind with truth in order to understand that those are merely opinions, and to remember that God's opinion is the only one that matters! Condemnation and shame are challenges you will face as a Christian in your life, and they will eventually make you stronger, wiser, and everything that God planned for you to be. The dangerous truth is that you can live a life of adventure when you realize that His challenges will only draw you closer to Him, make you stronger, and help you get out of the storm.

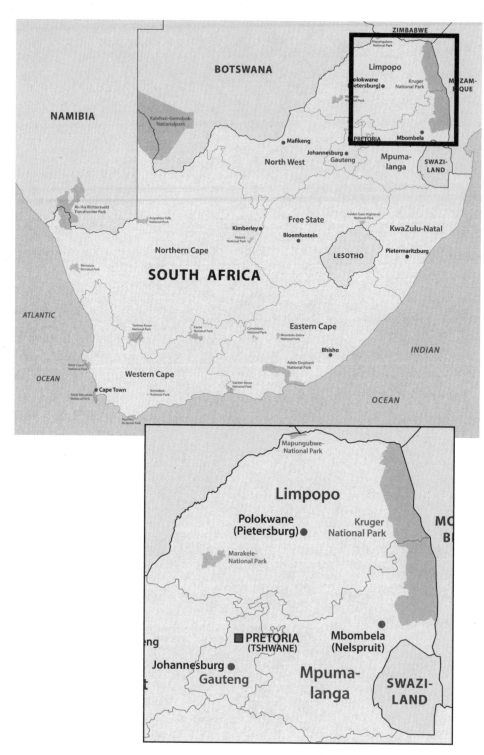

Kruger National Park

THE WILDS

WATCHING EACH OTHER'S BACKS

We arrived at our ranger walk trailhead just as the sun broke over the horizon. The Kruger National Park rangers quickly gathered us into a semicircle, and, in a hushed tone, began their orientation.

"If we say, 'Do not run' and you run, you will die. If we say, 'Get into a tree as quickly as you can' and you hesitate, you will die. End of orientation!"

That was it? End of orientation? My emotions were beginning to go on high alert.

It's important to understand something. Emotions, in and of themselves, are not bad things. They make us aware that something isn't right, or safe in this instance. Emotions can keep you from making a bad decision, such as running away, activating the prey drive in a predator, or they can help you make a good decision, such as climbing a tree, so that the predator's breath doesn't smell like you!

As we left the safety of the all-terrain vehicles and proceeded into the waist-high grass, our guides stopped to let us know they would be walking point (at the front) of our five-man team.

Here was their explanation: "Lions and leopards almost always attack from the front, so we will take the lead."

It was as if their words had made their way through my ear canals and sank deep into the pit of my stomach.

Almost always? I thought.

I turned to look behind me, and realized that I was the last man in line. If anything decided to attack from the rear, I was toast. I had a choice. I could either trust our guides and all their years of experience in the African bush, or spend the day constantly looking over my shoulder.

For the next four hours, we made our way through the tall grass, up boulder-strewn hillsides, across dried-up river beds covered with lion and rhino tracks, and across massive game trails. I was impressed as our guides easily identified every track, where the animals were headed, how old they were, and even if the animal was on the hunt. They had more than the hat and T-shirt, and they were equipped to guide us through the wilderness.

By about hour two of our trek, we stopped for a short snack. One of the rangers opened up a small Ziploc baggie and removed a piece of African jerky, or Biltong. Biltong is a variety of cured meat that originated in South Africa. Various types of meat are used to produce it, ranging from beef and game meats to fillets of ostrich from commercial farms. He tore off a chunk and passed it to me. The taste wasn't as sweet as what I was used to with American jerky.

He waited patiently for me to chew on it a while before he asked, "What do you think?"

I responded, "Is this kudu?"

With an ear-to-ear grin, he replied, "No, it is baboon testicle!"

Before my reflex muscle could dislodge the piece of meat from my throat, he began laughing, and said, "I am just kidding!"

Great sense of humor those African guides have.

About three hours into the walk, we came upon a dung pile that was literally two-thirds the size of a Volkswagen. Rhinos, in an effort to mark their territory, defecate in the same location, over and over, and they can produce up to fifty pounds of dung per day! A single rhino may have twenty to thirty of these piles to alert passing rhinoceroses that this is his area. In addition, an adult bull, while patrolling, will mark his territory by wiping his horns on bushes or the ground, and by scraping his feet before spraying urine up to ten times per hour in every direction. I stood in awe.

Heading back to where we'd parked, we came to a small field that stood between us and the Landcruiser. Halfway across the field, an adult male white rhino appeared in front of us. At first, we were elated! We hadn't seen any rhinos all day. Now, standing before us was a magnificent five-thousand-pound prehistoric monster. As I fumbled for my camera to record the moment, the beast, without warning, cut us off from returning to our vehicle.

I recalled a story shortly before we'd arrived in Kruger about a famous African veterinarian, who, while trying to shoot a rhino with a dart gun, was charged. He was gored in the thigh, his back was snapped, and he was tossed through the air and into a thorny Acacia tree, sticking to it as if he were attached by Velcro.

My thoughts and emotions were spiraling downward quickly.

This rhino clearly didn't like us being in his territory, and he was on a search-and-destroy mission. Rhinos can kill people. We knew that! When we thought there was a good possibility he was going to charge, a sudden avalanche of "fight or flight" washed over us. We were on an emotional rollercoaster.

Rhinos can't see worth squat, but with their overgrown nostrils and ears, you're in deep dung if they detect you or have their young with them. Adults can grow to be almost twelve feet in length and can be the weight of our Landcruiser. When spooked by an unfamiliar sound or smell, they are likely to charge. The other scary fact about rhinos is that they can run two to three times as fast as a human, so climbing a tree just may be your only escape if one charges. Because their eyesight is so poor (about 15 feet), standing motionless also may be your best option if you haven't already played your cards.

This rhino hadn't seen us but he'd gotten a nostril-full and was circling back and forth, trying to determine our position. There was only one tree in the field, and that became our newest best friend. The three of us who weren't used to being confronted with a five-thousand-pound freight train kept circling the tree and trying to hide. We must have looked like the Three Stooges. The two park rangers stood motionless, calmly and coolly instructing the rest of us to stand still. They kept their .458 Winchester

Magnums cradled, thumbs on the safety, fingers off the trigger, but at the ready should deadly force be needed. These Winchesters are belted, straight-taper-cased, dangerous game rifles that feel like mortars compared to most hunting rifles in the US. They can drop an elephant in its tracks, if warranted. The truth is, they definitely had the right weapon for the job, and they knew how to use them if circumstances called for lethal action.

The two rangers understood the consequences of allowing their emotions to cause fear and panic. We, on the other hand, were a walking billboard for unhealthy emotions. Basically, we were shouting, "Here I am! Come kill me!" The rangers could have made fun of us for being stupid Americans, but they never mocked us, talked down to us, or used shame and condemnation to move us to safety. We trusted them, and we moved when they said move. That's what it looks like to have a qualified guide leading you through the wilderness.

8

ACCOUNTABILITY

All that was heard was, "I'm done." That's what a man said as he walked out of the men's ministry breakfast. "I can't keep this up any longer. I'm going to screw up sometime today, tomorrow, next week, or next month. I'll never be good enough for you, and I'll never be good enough for God."

The room fell silent.

A church in Virginia had invited me to speak at a men's event the night before. They asked me to stay over for their men's breakfast and Sunday service to get a feel for how the men were involved in their church, outside of putting on the event. Most men love men's events. They love good food, they love adventure, they love to get away from their daily life, and they love to be entertained. They love to plan the events, be a part of the event, and get other guys pumped up to turn out. But after the event is over, to put it bluntly, men tend to disappear.

The event twelve hours earlier had attracted over six hundred men, 60 percent of whom did not attend the host church. That left around two hundred fifty men who I thought I'd see the following morning at church. Not even close.

I arrived at the church around 7:30 a.m., as the breakfast was to begin at 8:00. That morning, I was going to speak about who men really are, not the façade that so many of us have bought into for most of our lives. About ten minutes before I was to address the twenty or so men who showed up, the men's ministry leader invited me to pray with a couple of other men from the church. Then, he proceeded to fill me in on how they typically do their men's breakfasts. First, they pray. Then, they welcome the guys back, followed by another prayer, then a Scripture reading, and then they break into smaller accountability groups in which the elders of the church question the younger men about how they'd succeeded and failed the week before. Before the hour is up, any men who want to get up and confess their failures before the group are invited to do so.

I don't think he saw me cringe as he was speaking.

Things began as scheduled and proceeded as normal, followed by a tallying of how many men had received Christ at the event the night before. Fifty-two men had indicated on their response cards at the end of the evening that they'd received Christ, and another thirty-eight indicated that they were recommitting their lives to Christ. The handful of men in the room applauded, and the event was deemed a success.

As I stepped up to the microphone to address the men at that morning prayer breakfast, a list with bullet points caught my eye on the podium in front of me. It was a list of accountability questions they'd printed off the Internet that they were using to question each other for the purpose of becoming more Christ-like. Their intentions were noble, but their knowledge of transformation was only skin-deep. I took a minute to glance at each accountability facilitator's list. Here's what I saw:

FACILITATOR #1

+ Have you inappropriately touched a woman since we last met?

+ Have you viewed pornography in any form since we last met?

+ Have you had a regular time of personal worship in so far as your travel schedule and need for rest has allowed?

+ Have you had regular intercessional prayer time in so far as your travel schedule and need for rest has allowed?

+ Are you giving more than you're receiving?

+ Are the "visible" you and the "real" you consistent?

+ Have any of your financial dealings lacked integrity in any way?

+ Have you been faithful in sharing your faith this week?

+ Have you begun each day with prayer? If so, for how long?

+ Do you pray continuously?

+ Do you save pennies?

+ Does your penny jar weigh more than a book?

+ Did your driving set an example for others?

+ Have you lied to me?

FACILITATOR #2

+ Have you had a consistent time of Bible reading and prayer?

+ Have you looked at pornography in any form?

+ Have you looked at a woman inappropriately?

+ Is there anyone to whom you have been disrespectful?

+ Have you been spending enough time with your wife?

+ Are you keeping up with paying your bills on time?

+ Does your life reflect verbal integrity?

+ Have you been knowingly disobedient to the Lord in any way?

+ Have you fulfilled the mandates of your calling?

+ Are you giving to the Lord's work financially? If so, what percentage of your income?

+ Are you spending time memorizing and dwelling on Scripture?

+ If so, have them quote the Scripture they've memorized.

+ Have you supported a local charity?

+ Do you brush and floss after every meal?

+ Do you exercise daily for one hour continuously?

+ Have you lied?

Even looking at these lists now creates a twinge in my eye, and even worse, makes me want to stick my finger down my throat to purge myself of decades of shame and condemnation men have suffered at the hands of well-meaning yet ignorant believers. It reeks of religion, lactates legalism, and injects a Botox shot of outward behavior modification into the soul of the believer, in the belief that looking good equals being good.

The bloodstream and veins of the church, which once flowed deep with Christ-centered transformation through Holy Spirit revelation, have collapsed. The body of Christ has become spiritually dehydrated from the lack of believers who would bring hope and encouragement through the life-giving water of Christ's gift on the cross. Good men are collapsing, exhausted beneath the weight of sin management, as the only man who could possibly bear the penalty of sin's shame already hung on that cross.

Many religious, banner-waving accountability flag-bearers are fostering an unholy fear of God through the lens of shame and condemnation, in an attempt to right a ship that sank, and was resurrected long ago without any additional assistance from man. Accountability, in its worst form, dilutes, masks, and attempts to wash away the blood-stained wood with the sweat of our brow, yank out the love-filled nails forged in grace and forgiveness, and attempts to replace them with the spackling of human effort in a vain attempt to appease an angry judge and a self-righteous jury.

Any attempt through my works to create sanctification, or by demanding that others conform to a works-based accountability program with the purpose of creating man-made sanctification, in essence, is spitting on the cross, and committing adultery against Jesus Christ. It's not that the above list is bad—it's not. Those are all worthy goals to aspire to. But if the goal is to "clean up your act" so that your life will be acceptable to God and to others, and not to "know God more," you're never going to experience and embrace the love and grace that creates real transformation, that creates the kind of trust in other men that leads to a Christ-centered, holy life.

The apostle Paul knew that "rule keeping" to please God and others doesn't work. Look at this passage we explored earlier in Galatians 2:19–21 (MSG):

> *What actually took place is this: I tried keeping rules and working my head off to please God, and it didn't work. So I quit being a "law man" so that I could be God's man. Christ's life showed me how, and enabled me to do it. I identified myself completely with him. Indeed, I have been crucified with Christ. My ego is no longer central. It is no longer important that I appear righteous before you or have your good opinion, and I am no longer driven to impress God. Christ lives in me. The*

life you see me living is not "mine," but it is lived by faith in the Son of God, who loved me and gave himself for me. I am not going to go back on that. Is it not clear to you that to go back to that old rule-keeping, peer-pleasing religion would be an abandonment of everything personal and free in my relationship with God? I refuse to do that, to repudiate God's grace. If a living relationship with God could come by rule-keeping, then Christ died unnecessarily. (MSG)

The accountability model of life transformation is horribly broken, ineffective, insufficient, and driving men into hiding in massive numbers, creating a void of male leaders, mentors, husbands, and fathers. In many ways, Christian accountability is attempting to create another savior—us.

The truth is that if I could manage all this stuff on my own through simply trying harder, there would be no need for a Savior. Nowhere in Scripture does it say that it's my job to make you confess your sins to me. *"Confessing…sins to one another"* (James 5:16) is biblical and essential, but if we mandate the practice through shame, condemnation, and pressure to "come clean," and without the element of relational trust, men are doomed.

The most dangerous aspect of accountability is that even when it works, it creates pride, judgment, arrogance, and a mind-set that says, "I'm better than you." This is exactly why Jesus nailed the Pharisees about their attitudes in keeping the law.

[Jesus] *replied* [to the Pharisees and teachers of the law], *"Isaiah was right when he prophesied about you hypocrites; as it is written: 'These people honor me with their lips, but their hearts are far from me. They worship me in vain; their teachings are merely human rules.'"*
(Mark 7:6–7)

The Pharisees were bent on cleansing the outside of the cup and dish, whereas the inside remained filthy. Jesus even compared their own insides to *"whitewashed tombs"* that were full of corruption:

Woe to you, teachers of the law and Pharisees, you hypocrites! You are like whitewashed tombs, which look beautiful on the outside, but on the inside are full of the bones of the dead and everything unclean. In the same way, on the outside you appear to people as righteous but on the inside you are full of hypocrisy and wickedness. (Matthew23:27–28)

Outward self-righteousness is what comes from pharisaic legalism. Jesus revealed their true hearts and motives: *"Everything they do is done for people to see"* (verse 5).

So then, if holding others accountable creates pride and self-righteousness, who are we to be accountable to?

It's God we are answerable to—all the way from life to death and everything in between—not each other. That's why Jesus lived and died and then lived again: so that he could be our Master across the entire range of life and death, and free us from the petty tyrannies of each other. (Romans 14:8–9 MSG)

Here's the same chapter in the *New Living Translation*:

So why do you condemn another believer? Why do you look down on another believer? Remember, we will all stand before the judgment seat of God. For the Scriptures say, "As surely as I live," says the LORD, "every knee will bend to me, and every tongue will declare allegiance to God." Yes, each of us will give a personal account to God. So let's stop condemning each other. Decide instead to live in such a way that you will not cause another believer to stumble and fall. (verses 10–13)

Here is the same passage in *The Message*:

So where does that leave you when you criticize a brother? And where does that leave you when you condescend to a sister? I'd say it leaves you looking pretty silly—or worse. Eventually, we're all going to end up kneeling side by side in the place of judgment, facing God. Your critical and condescending ways aren't going to improve your position there one bit. Read it for yourself in Scripture: "As I live and breathe," God says, 'every knee will bow before me; every tongue will tell the honest truth that I and only I am God." So tend to your knitting. You've got your hands full just taking care of your own life before God. Forget about deciding what's right for each other. Here's what you need to be concerned about: that you don't get in the way of someone else, making life more difficult than it already is.

But isn't it my job to correct my brother and hold him accountable when he steps out of line? Look at Romans 14:4:

If there are corrections to be made or manners to be learned, God can handle that without your help. (MSG)

Whenever I have the honor of speaking for a men's retreat, how to properly hold each other accountable is one of the top issues men want to understand. Here is how I respond: "I want you to imagine that each of you has an addiction. It could be porn, drugs, alcohol, anger, eating...whatever. Now, what could another person do that would keep you from sharing what's really happening in your life with them and building a relationship of trust?"

The men always begin shouting out their responses:

"Judging me."

"Trying to fix me."

"Shaming me."

"Gossiping and telling others about me."

"Throwing Scripture at me."

"Condemning me, using fear and guilt."

I then ask them, "Does that move you closer to them, or further away?"

Their response is always, "Further away."

"Then tell me what a person could do that would help to build a relationship of trust in which you would feel safe to tell them everything that's really going on in your life?"

This response always takes time, as they've never been asked this before. It's not been modeled for them. Eventually, they began to open up and responds.

"Listen to me, first."

"Try to empathize with me."

"Ask me questions about my life."

"Speak the truth to me, but don't remove your love and acceptance from me."

"Spend time with me. Get into my world."

"Seek to understand me before being understood yourself."

"Really get to know me without having the agenda of trying to fix me."

Which of these ways is more effective when it comes to accountability? By giving men a list of do's and don'ts coated in shame, condemnation, fear, and performance? Or by loving them right where they are, by finding the truth in what they're saying, by entering into their pain, by asking questions and learning along with them, and by allowing the Holy Spirit to direct the conversation?

BUILDING TRUST

There are three things you can do that will greatly help you build trust with the men around you, so that an atmosphere of safety and accountability can be created. Since we used TEA earlier, let's keep it simple and use those same letters:

1. **Truth** – Find "some" truth in what they are saying, no matter how small it may seem. It's very real to them.

2. **Empathy** – Enter into their pain with them, not to enable them but to help them understand that you truly care about them. Repeat and rephrase what they've said. This lets them know that you've heard what they're saying. Jesus was the master at this.

3. **Ask questions** – Get into their world by asking questions to help them discover what's creating their unhealthiness.

I was an eighteen-year-old kid, fresh out of high school and living in Emporium, Pennsylvania. I had been made the manager of a shoe store three hours away from my hometown. That was a lot of responsibility for a young kid who hadn't tasted a lot of real life yet. I was working seventy hours a week, missing my parents, my friends, and my girlfriend of two years. Suddenly, I was put in charge of tens of thousands of dollars in inventory. It was as if my head was a pressure-cooker and there was no pressure release valve. I was about to explode!

On a weekend in early September, a buddy of mine drove the three-hour trip to pay me a visit. He brought with him some things he thought would cheer me up: two six-packs of beer, a box of cigars, and a couple of porn magazines.

I had grown up in a home where there was no drinking, no smoking, and definitely no porn! We went to church on Wednesday night and twice on Sunday. My father taught Sunday school and was an elder in the church, and my mother was the choir director. We looked "good."

When my friend pulled out the stash he'd brought for me, at first, I didn't know what to do. After all, my friend was popular in the high school we attended together, and I wanted to be popular and accepted as well.

Should I tell him not to bring it into my house? If I did that, I was afraid he might think that I was judging him, or that he might think I wasn't "cool," or that I would seem ungrateful for his effort to cheer me up. If I did let him bring it in, I was worried about what my parents might think if they found out.

After the first couple of beers, the rest, unfortunately, came too easy. My judgment began to become compromised, along with my core beliefs. I began to be lured into Satan's lies, and was soon injected with his deadly toxin: I forget who I truly was.

As my inhibitions faded, we began to fill the room with bottle caps and smoke. My fingers began leaping through the pages like a kid digging into a candy jar. After two days of "debauching," my friend left for home, leaving his "gifts" behind as well. Needless to say, I didn't feel too good.

The following Monday morning at work, the delivery truck showed up right on time, 6:00 a.m., unloading dozens of heavy boxes that I had sort, price, and stock by nine o'clock. My head was hurting, I was disappointed in myself, and a steady swarm of customers began filing in around the lunch hour. I was standing behind the cash register, attempting to inhale a sandwich as the last customer went out the door, when the door suddenly opened again. Walking in with huge smiles on their faces were my parents. My parents? Wait…my parents!

I swallowed hard, and the next few words came out of my mouth, like choking on my tuna on rye sandwich. "Hi, what…what are you doing here?"

"Well, we thought we'd surprise you by waiting for you in your apartment," my father exclaimed, "but when we got there, the door was locked."

"Oh, that's too bad," I said, swallowing hard and trying to hide the beads of sweat breaking out on my forehead.

My mother looked at me, and said, "You don't look too good, son. Why don't you give us the keys, and we'll go to your house, cook supper, and do a little cleaning before you get home."

Thoughts began racing through my mind. Maybe they hadn't looked through the window, but then again, maybe they had! Should I come clean and tell them of my ungodly debauchery? The beads of sweat were quickly becoming rivers of repentance.

In those moments, it's funny the kind of prayers we come up with: "Dear God, holy and magnificent One, if You somehow, in Your heart of hearts, could ever see fit to have mercy on your child who really messed up and is deeply sorry, now would be a *really* good time! I promise to become an advocate against the things of the flesh, to admonish those who aren't walking in your way. Holy and most high and everlasting Father, I'll even go to church four times a week if You can hide my wrong-doing just this one time. Please, oh please, oh please!"

Having been brought up in a somewhat legalistic, performance-based church, one Bible verse kept going through my head: *"But if ye will not do so, behold, ye have sinned against the* Lord: *and be sure your sin will find you out"* (Numbers 32:23 kjv, of course). That verse turned my sweaty river of repentance into a deluge of despair!

In that moment, I did the only thing a scared eighteen-year-old kid knew to do: "Run, Forrest, run!" I handed the store keys to the assistant manager, told my parents to give me five minutes to unlock the door and tidy up a bit, jumped into my souped-up 1975 Pontiac Firebird, raced down Main Street like it was the final lap of the Indy 500, ran up the stairs to my apartment, threw open the door, and began tossing my debauchery into a thirty-gallon plastic trash bag. I even burned a couple of pieces of toast to cover up the smell of beer and cigars. Don't get any ideas, young men!

As I was placing the last clue from the crime scene into the trash bag, the door opened.

"Hey, son, why don't you let me help carry that trash downstairs for you?"

"Thanks, Dad," I replied. The sweat on my forehead and the red in my cheeks were now dissipating, as I was sure I'd just gotten a "get-out-of-jail-free card"! I invited them all the way in and, after a while, enjoyed a home-cooked meal for the first time in several months.

The next morning, I was awakened by the fragrant smell of Maxwell House coffee brewing, and the sound of sizzling French toast cooking in the kitchen. It was a good morning to be alive! God had heard my prayers and had mercy on me.

As I walked into the kitchen, my mother greeted me with one of my favorite phrases, "Are you hungry?"

I smiled, and said, "Yes, I am!"

As she handed me a plate and filled my mug with coffee, I asked, "Where's Dad?"

I will never forget the next sentence as long as I live.

"Oh, you won't believe this. Sometime last night, a dog must have torn open the trash bags, and your garbage is scattered all over the lawn. Relax. Your father is down there cleaning up the mess."

Relax? Something powerful happens when you've finally been caught in your sin. Maybe not at first, but when the truth is finally out and you're no longer hiding your "stuff," it's like a dam opening and releasing all that pent-up pressure. As I made my way down the outer stairs, there he was, picking up my garbage—my sin.

I was so ashamed.

What happened next changed my life forever. He didn't say what I expected, which would have been something along the lines of, "I can't believe you did this! What were you thinking? What would your mother think if she saw this? Do you know how this could ruin your witness?" He also didn't withdraw from me, rub my nose in it, or give any emotional, knee-jerk consequences. All he did was start out by asking me a simple question without condemnation.

"Are you doing okay?"

It was obvious I wasn't, but he was more concerned about me than he was about my sin.

What I received from him was genuine concern. His tender, guiding hands alongside mine, helping to clean up my mess and asking nonjudgmental questions, without removing his love from me. In that moment, I knew it was safe to open up, and share the pain I'd been going through, which then led to the discovery of why I'd acted out in the first place.

My father knew the power in walking with me rather than doing what Satan was attempting to do—condemning me. Why? He understood the difference between condemnation and conviction. He knew that, as a believer, I was already being convicted by the Holy Spirit. As I said earlier, condemnation leads to shame, hiding, and more unhealthy actions, but the Holy Spirit's conviction always leads to repentance and obedience. My father knew that if there were manners to be learned or corrections to be made, God could handle all of that without his help. My father knew who I truly was in Christ and he honored me by allowing the Holy Spirit's revelation to convict me while not removing his own love from me. He helped me throw my sin in the trash, which is where it belonged in the first place.

In that moment, I began to understand the power of asking the right questions. I also learned the difference between condemnation and conviction. Instead of being driven deeper into my shame and feeling the need to hide my sin, his quiet love built a foundation of trust, in which I realized that he loved me more than he hated the sin. My wanting to do what was right and pleasing before God greatly increased, and my urge to rebel decreased.

"SHOULDING" ON YOURSELF

The enemy is a liar who loves to "should" on us. What I mean is that he loves to use "should" statements to try to get us to perform for our worth.

You should be smarter.

You should have more money.

You should get into better shape.

You should, you should, you should….

The enemy spends most of his energy "shoulding" on us, and we buy into it. It's as silent as a hunter's arrow and deadly as a viper bite. All of these "shoulds" work to push you toward every identity but your own. Be accountable for you who you really are in Christ. Be thankful for your shortcomings, for they are really blessings. They make you humble, approachable, desirable, and relatable.

So, how do we truly help men walk with God without giving them a long performance-based "to-do" list, and without trying to fix and control them? It's exactly what we've been discovering, and the foundation's built on helping them understand their true identity: "Christ in me!"

The writer Paul penned some foundational truth in Romans 8:16. He wrote, "God's Spirit touches our Spirit and confirms who we really are. We know who he is, and we know who we are: Father and children." If we believe God's Word, that we are His children, deeply loved, totally forgiven, and that we have the Holy Spirit in us, why would we waste valuable time thinking about other people's opinions of us? Why would we waste time entertaining the need to perform for our worth? When we belong to Him, we are already pleasing to God—just the way we are. He can't love us any more than He already does. We don't have to carry the shame of the enemy's lies any longer.

Just as my father helped me throw my garbage and debauchery to the curb, but still moved me to be accountable before God for my actions by loving me and asking questions, our heavenly Father's Word throws the enemy's lies out with the trash, once and for all! The truth is that you are accountable for your sin. You are responsible for your actions, and while God forgives them "seventy times seven" times (Matthew 18:22), you've got to get to a point where you realize that you can't blame others for your sins. You are responsible. You are accountable. And God, through His loving kindness, will move you into authentic repentance. It's a beautiful thing.

INTO THE WILDS FIELD GUIDE

CHAPTER EIGHT: ACCOUNTABILITY

What if there was a place so safe that the worst of me could be
known, and I would discover that I would not be loved less,
but more in the telling of it?
—*John Lynch*, The Cure

That's a powerful statement. Isn't that what we all long for—the way
we know at our core it should be? Shouldn't we be able to confess our sins,
and process our issues with others, without feeling as though we're report-
ing to a parole officer? Unfortunately, all the "to do" lists, and all the hoops
men have been required to jump through, often by ignorant believers trying to force confessions out of them, have created an environment of shame
and worthlessness, causing men to leave churches in droves as a result.

Confessing sin is a healthy thing. James 5:16 tells us that we are to
confess our sins one to another so that we can be healed. When we have a
safe place to confess our sins, trust is built and burdens are lifted. But when
we throw condemnation, guilt, and shame on each other, not to mention
heaping piles of "should" (i.e., you *should* have known better; you *should*
love your wife as Christ loved the church; you *should* tithe more), trust is
destroyed. If God doesn't do that to us, why do we feel the need to do it to
each other?

Read the following Scripture:

*It's God we are answerable to—all the way from life to death and ev-
erything in between—not each other. That's why Jesus lived and died
and then lived again: so that he could be our Master across the entire
range of life and death, and free us from the petty tyrannies of each
other.*   (Romans 14:8–9 MSG)

1.   According to this passage, who we are accountable to?

2.   What do you think Paul means when he writes, "*...and free us from the petty tyrannies of each other*"?

Accountability is a good thing, but it can't be forced. The one who is confessing must be ready and desire to confess. He must see the need for it; otherwise, it's just conformity.

3.   Where does revelation come from, and when does it happen?

Whenever we try to "get someone" to do anything, what is usually the response? They want to rebel. We know that revelation comes from God, and it happens when He knows we're ready to receive it. Otherwise, we would choose to stay stuck in our unhealthiness, because sin can be so attractive. The beautiful thing is this: *grace* is more attractive than *sin*.

Whenever I hear someone say, "That's just cheap grace," it breaks my heart. It means they don't understand grace.

Grace always leads to obedience, or it's not grace.

Remember that. Write it down. Paste it to your forehead, if you need to. It's grace that leads us to the love of the Father, not fear and shame.

Take a look at this passage from Romans 2:4:

Or do you think lightly of the riches of His kindness and tolerance and patience, not knowing that the kindness of God leads you to repentance?   (NASB)

4.   According to that verse, what leads us to repentance? What does this verse have to say about that?

Repentance isn't about groveling or showing enough tears and remorse to please God—or others. *Repentance* means "to change the way you think." God convicts us, but He never condemns us. The Greek word for *repent* is *metanoeo*, meaning "to change your mind." Biblical repentance involves a change of mind, or a change in how we think. What do we change our minds about? We change our minds about our sin, and about our own ability to satisfy the demands of God's righteousness. We agree with God that we need His righteousness, because *"all our righteous acts are like filthy rags"* (Isaiah 64:6). Yet many Christians demand that others follow a "to do" list in order to become "accepted" and "worthy." That is not the message of the gospel.

Nowhere in Scripture does it say that it's my job to force you, or "get you," to repent. Repentance happens when we understand that we can't *earn* God's grace. It's not something we can buy, barter for, or earn. God isn't some genie in a lamp who will grant our wish for grace if we only rub the lamp enough times (i.e. keep the law). Grace comes because of Jesus's gift on the cross to save us from *all* our sins, not just a select few sins.

Read the following verses:

For God sent not his Son into the world to condemn the world; but that the world through him might be saved. (John 3:17 KJV)

Then he said, "Look, I have come to do your will." He cancels the first covenant in order to put the second into effect. For God's will was for us to be made holy by the sacrifice of the body of Jesus Christ, once for all time. (Hebrews 10:9–10 NLT)

Therefore there is now no condemnation for those who are in Christ Jesus. (Romans 8:1 NASB)

This righteousness from God comes through faith in Jesus Christ to all and over all who believe. In fact, there is no difference, because all have sinned and fall short of the glory of God and are justified freely by his grace through the redemption that is in Christ Jesus. (Romans 3:22–24 EHV)

If there are corrections to be made or manners to be learned, God can handle that without your help. (Romans 14:4 MSG)

5. Throughout these verses, what repeating themes do think God is trying to communicate to us as believers?

6. If you truly believe that God is not condemning you, and that Jesus died for *all* of your sins, would that cause you be drawn to Him more, or less? Why?

7. If you understood that there is nothing you can do that would make God love you more, and nothing you can do that would make Him love you less, what would that realization do to your relationship with Him? Would you be as hesitant to confess your sins?

I want you to imagine for a moment that you have an addiction. In truth, you do have an addciton, but it's not something you might recognize as destructive, like watching too much TV, being too attached to your cell phone, or eating too much. I want you to think of an addiction that you see as being really bad. Got it?

8. What could someone else do or say that *would not* be helpful to you in moving past your addiction?

9. What could someone else do or say that *would* be helpful to you in moving past your addiction?

10. Why do you think people often use shaming, shunning, judging, and/or condemning to get others to change their behavior or repent from sin? Do you think this affects how "condemned" people view God?

Reread the quote from the beginning of this segment.

> What if there was a place so safe that the worst of me could be
> known, and I would discover that I would not be loved less,
> but more in the telling of it?
> —*John Lynch*, The Cure

That is when true accountability happens. That's what it looks like. "*Iron sharpens iron, so one man sharpens another*" (Proverbs 27:17 NASB). The truth is, if I could manage all this stuff on my own by "trying harder," I would have no need for a Savior. Confessing our sins "one to another" is biblical and critical, but whenever shame, condemnation, and pressure to "come clean" become the driving force, without the element of relational trust, men are doomed. Men, it's time to draw our swords and do battle against the true enemy—the "father of lies." Our fight is not with each other. Fight well.

9

MY BEAUTIFUL SHIPWRECK

Consider it pure joy, my brothers and sisters, whenever you face trials of many kinds, because you know that the testing of your faith produces perseverance. Let perseverance finish its work so that you may be mature and complete, not lacking anything. (James 1:2–4)

One of the most powerful concepts in this book is something I've learned to affectionately call "Challenges are Gifts." In other words, those tough things we face are actually what my grandmother used to call "blessings in disguise." As a young man, I used to think she sounded trite and flippant when she said that. Now that I've gone through many trials of my own, I understand just how true and powerful that phrase really is.

Several years ago, I was sitting at a restaurant having breakfast with a close friend, Kurt. He is a very smart and successful businessman. At the time we met, he had a 7,200-square-foot home, made more money in a week than I make in a year, and, in my estimation, was living a life that most men would envy.

As I washed down my ritual bowl of oatmeal with a cup of coffee, he was doing the same with steak and eggs. At some point during our conversation, he began to get emotional, so I asked him what was up.

"Brent," he said, "I've made a lot of money—so much money that I decided to try my hand in another business. But only eighteen months in to this new endeavor, I nearly lost it all. My new business crashed and burned, and it took nearly every asset in my other business to keep me from going under."

Tears began to well up in his eyes.

"I felt so bad about myself," he continued, "that I set up a meeting with my pastor to confess how poorly I was doing, and how much of a failure I was. What he told me changed my life, and that's why I'm getting emotional right now. Honestly, I was expecting a big lecture from my pastor, maybe something about how I brought this on myself by being greedy, but he only asked me one question: 'Kurt, were you closer to God when you were making money hand-over-fist, or were you closer to Him when you nearly lost it all?' It didn't take long for me to come up with an answer. I told him I had been closer to God when I nearly lost it all. My pastor looked at me, smiled, and said, 'Then, my friend, that's not a failure…that's a huge success!'"

THE GIFT OF FAILURE

I recalled that I had heard my pastor once say, "God cares more about your character than He cares about your comfort." The Scriptures are full of people whose lives "hit bottom." Noah, Moses, Abraham, David, Job, Stephen, Paul—the list goes on. In chapter 3, I highlighted something called "The Big Lie": My performance + others' opinions = my self-worth. That's the same lie that sunk Adam and Eve, and it was the same lie that almost took down my friend Kurt.

Failure can cause us to question our worth. When we look to anyone or anything else to get our worth, we are attempting to draw water from a dry well. God is the only One who can give us living water, and in His incredible love for His children, He wants us to not only read about Him, sing about Him, and talk about Him, but to know Him as Abba, Father, especially when no one is looking. Failure is essential to our maturity. It is a gift.

One of the greatest moments of my life was when I had the opportunity to baptize both of my children. Knowing they are filled with the Holy Spirit brings me great joy and peace. As their father, if I bail them out of the consequences of their bad choices every time they make a mistake, they'll never learn how to stand on their own. They'll become dependent on me, and I desperately want them to know that they already have within them what it takes to make good choices—the leading of the Holy Spirit. If I hold them accountable instead of bailing them out, I'm helping them grow up. Even though to them it may feel as though I've pulled the rug out from under them, I love them more by keeping them from becoming completely dependent on me or any other person. Shielding a child from consequences when they disobey (without the emotional shaming and blaming, of course) is as debilitating to them as it would be to hit them across the shins with a baseball bat to keep them from walking. Love can be defined as "doing what's best for another person's spiritual growth."

God wants us to rely on Him, not pat advice from well-meaning spouses, parents, or friends. You can be respectful and listen to what they have to say, but your full reliance should be on the Lord.

Look at this verse from Psalm 146:3–4:

Don't put your life in the hands of experts who know nothing of life, of salvation life. Mere humans don't have what it takes; when they die, their projects die with them.   (MSG)

I don't think anyone wants to hit bottom, but it happens to the best of us. Sometimes it takes hitting bottom in your career, your marriage, your physical health, or through the loss of a loved one for us to go to the next level of spiritual development. Many of our circumstances have left us asking, "Why do bad things happen to good people?" Inevitably, we all will face challenges that, if we allow them to, will make us better people. And in truth, bad things *do* happen to good people, and sometimes, good people make poor choices that create their difficult circumstances.

Years ago, I made a poor choice by getting too close to a woman I was working with. My marriage had been struggling, and I had bought into the lie that my wife should be able to meet all my emotional needs. When those hidden expectations weren't met, I bought into another lie the enemy was whispering in my ear: "You deserve to be treated better." That lie hurt a lot of people, and almost cost me my marriage. Even though the emotional relationship was never extended outside the workplace, it was still sin.

That time was undoubtedly the worst experience I've ever gone through. My thoughts caused me a lot of guilt and shame, and my emotions were dragged into a dark hole. I hit bottom...hard. Why? Because I forgot I was already 100 percent complete in Christ.

For months, I prayed and pleaded with God to remove this pain, to somehow make it all just a bad dream—but He didn't do that. He had another plan, a plan to allow me to hit bottom, a place where my to-do lists wouldn't cut it, a place so desolate that only His loving arms would be able to pull me up from the depths.

What I didn't expect was that years later, I'd be writing this story in a book, or that I would one day be able to thank God for those circumstances. Today, I can honestly say that I wouldn't trade what God has done in me and in my marriage through those circumstances for anything in the world! I call it "my beautiful shipwreck."

In the years that followed my shipwreck, God threw me a lifeline through some amazing men who have helped to guide me through the spiritual wilderness, as well as the actual physical wilderness. They taught me how to survive not only the unforgiving environments of places like Africa and Alaska, but also right here on the home front, my own household. These men are my workout and hunting buddies, fellow adventurers, safe sounding boards, and brothers in Christ. These men have their own lies that they believe and wrestle with, but when they engage with each other through their own true identity, they are dangerous for good!

HITTING BOTTOM

When my son, Garrett, was just seven years old, I took him on a fishing trip. The stream we were fishing was swollen after four days of torrential rains, and we found ourselves stranded on a small rock island in the middle of the raging waters. Knowing we couldn't stay there long, I came up with a plan to leave my son on the island, move upstream to find a safe passage back across the water, and then to return to the island and lead my son across the swiftly moving waters.

In the rapids just above us was an eighteen-foot-deep whirlpool where two small streams merged. My idea was to get above the whirlpool, since two streams should be shallower than one. As I moved above the churning whirlpool, I took one step forward. My foot landed on a moss-covered rock beneath the dark, roiling waters, and instantly my legs were swept out from beneath me, and I was pulled into the revolving current of the whirlpool. I was quickly sucked to the bottom, and swept across partially submerged treetops, cartwheeling in the current as if being tossed by the power of a huge wave. I was disoriented and couldn't tell which way was up. My body slammed against a large rock at the bottom of a deep hole, and I was finally able to plant my feet on something solid and push off.

When my face finally broke the surface, I backstroked as hard as I could to the spot where my son was now standing. We both began yelling at the top of our lungs for help. Within ten minutes, three men were there to help us across to safety. When we arrived back at the truck, we both thanked God for sending us three "guardian angels."

I'd told that story countless times, and was about to put it in a book I was working on when a man who'd been mentoring me asked me a simple question: Was it a good thing or a bad thing that you hit bottom in that stream?

At first, I thought he was crazy.

"Weren't you listening?" I asked. "It was horrible! I almost drowned!"

Then he said, "You said this whirlpool was eighteen-feet deep. So what would have happened if you'd only been sucked down to twelve feet, six feet, or just one foot in that whirlpool?"

I thought for a moment, and then said, "I'd have drowned."

He asked again, "So, was it a good thing or a bad thing you hit bottom?"

Somewhere along the way, the enemy has convinced us that "hitting bottom" is a bad thing. When we see people about to have a personal shipwreck, we tend to jump in and try to "fix them." The truth is, until that person hits whatever bottom is facing them, the truth will never sink in. And without God's truth revealed in their life, they will just keep sinking.

The late Watchman Nee relates a story from one of his experiences as a Christian leader in Communist China. A group of young Christian brothers were gathered together to swim in one of the many creeks that run throughout the countryside there. Since most were not good swimmers, they were careful to remain close to the banks, so they would not get into water that was over their heads. One of the brothers went out a little too far and began to struggle in the deep water. Realizing his predicament, he began to cry out to his neighbors, who, by now, were out of the water and drying off.

"Help! Save me!" he yelled, thrashing his arms and legs in a futile attempt to keep his head above water.

Brother Nee knew that only one man—a lifeguard—was experienced enough at swimming to provide assistance, and he turned to him for help. Strangely enough, however, the would-be rescuer calmly watched the man's plight but made no move to save him, to the great consternation of Brother Nee and the rest of the group.

"Why don't you do something?" they all pleaded.

But the man just stood there, apparently unconcerned. After a few moments, the drowning man could stay afloat no more. His arms and legs grew tired and limp, and he began to sink beneath the surface of the water. Finally, the slow-moving lifeguard dove into the creek, and, with a few quick strokes, reached the victim and pulled him to safety.

Once all was well, Brother Nee was beside himself.

"I have never seen a Christian who loved his own life quite as much as you," he said to the lifeguard. "How could you stand by and watch your brother drown, ignoring his cries for help and prolonging his suffering?"

The lifeguard calmly explained, "If I were to jump in immediately and try to save a drowning man, he would clutch me in panic and pull me under with him. In order to be saved, he must come to the end of himself, and cease struggling to save himself. Only then can he be helped."

Ask yourself this question: *Is getting to the end of my rope a bad thing?*

If you answered, "yes," list the reasons why you believe that. What are you afraid of? What does it reveal about your trust in God? What notions do you hold about your own ability to save yourself?

If you answered, "no," list the reasons why you believe that. What does getting to the end of your rope mean to you? Does the end of your rope move you further away from God, or does it bring you closer to Him? Does it cause you to trust God more or less?

If you listen to a lot of the TV evangelists, you'd think hitting bottom was a bad thing. You'll even hear some say that God wants to bless you, meaning that He wants to give you finances, good health, a beautiful wife, a better job, obedient kids, and so on. But to fully understand what Jesus said about blessings, let's go back to the Sermon on the Mount:

You're blessed when you're at the end of your rope. With less of you there is more of God and his rule. You're blessed when you feel you've lost what is most dear to you. Only then can you be embraced by the One most dear to you You're blessed when you're content with just who you are—no more, no less. That's the moment you find yourselves proud owners of everything that can't be bought.

(Matthew 5:3–5 MSG)

The apostle Paul, who we've talked about several times in this book, had a *"handicap,"* or in other translations, a *"thorn in the flesh."* We don't know what that handicap was, but we know it was something that was visible to others. Why did God allow someone as educated and well-known as Paul was in his day to have a handicap, especially when he was destined to become one of the greatest voices of his day, next to Jesus, and author of the majority of the New Testament?

Look again at how Paul viewed his handicap:

Because of the extravagance of those revelations, and so I wouldn't get a big head, I was given the gift of a handicap to keep me in constant touch with my limitations. Satan's angel did his best to get me down; what he in fact did was push me to my knees. No danger then of walking around high and mighty! At first I didn't think of it as a gift, and begged God to remove it. Three times I did that, and then he told me, "My grace is enough; it's all you need. My strength comes into its own in your weakness." Once I heard that, I was glad to let it happen. I quit focusing on the handicap and began appreciating the gift. It was a case of Christ's strength moving in on my weakness. Now I take limitations in stride, and with good cheer, these limitations that cut me down to size—abuse, accidents, opposition, bad breaks. I just let Christ take over! And so the weaker I get, the stronger I become.

(2 Corinthians 12:7–10 MSG)

Paul saw his challenges as gifts. They kept him humble and caused him to rely more on God. Through the storm, he came to the revelation that God's grace was all he needed, and then he actually began to appreciate the gifts!

God wants us to deeply understand that "Christ in us" is the only thing that can complete us, satisfy our wants and desires, and turn challenges into gifts. Then, like Paul, we will be made *"fit for the kingdom."*

> *All this trouble is a clear sign that God has decided to make you fit for the kingdom.* (2 Thessalonians 1:5 MSG)

INTO THE WILDS FIELD GUIDE

CHAPTER NINE: MY BEAUTIFUL SHIPWRECK

Consider it pure joy, my brothers and sisters, whenever you face trials of many kinds, because you know that the testing of your faith develops perseverance. Let perseverance finish its work so that you may be mature and complete, not lacking anything.   (James 1:2–4)

Hitting bottom is not something that anyone prays for. Seriously, how many of us pray, "God, I'd like to be in a horrific car wreck today"? Or "Please allow me to have cancer"? Or "I'd like my wife to have an affair with my best friend"?

Nobody in their right mind prays for those kinds of personal shipwrecks.

We know that stuff happens that we can't control. Challenges hit us in every area of our lives. So, how do we handle it when we have those shipwrecks that cause not just physical pain, but also loss, grief, worry, shame, doubt, or fear?

One of my favorite quotes is "Adventure begins when plans go bad." In this final chapter, I tell the story of how I almost drowned, and that hitting bottom was the only thing that saved me. Had I been sucked down only a few feet into the whirlpool, I wouldn't have hit the bottom, from which I was able to push off and get back to the surface. Not hitting bottom would have assured my death. God allowed me to have an "a-ha!" moment that radically changed my thinking.

One of the most powerful concepts in this book involves a concept I've learned to affectionately call "challenges are gifts." It's all about identifying those blessings in disguise. In those moments when things hit the fan, we usually aren't able to recognize the gift within the challenge.

1.   Write about a personal crisis you've recently gone through, and the emotions you experienced as a result.

2. What were you thinking at that time that caused you to feel those emotions? Write out those thoughts.

3. What did you believe about your situation that shaped your thinking?

4. Can you identify the lies that came from your unhealthy belief system? What were they?

Remember, we know our thoughts are unhealthy when the emotions they produce line up with the deeds of the flesh. Healthy thoughts produce the fruits of the Spirit. (See Galatians 5:19–23.)

5. Regarding the personal crisis you wrote about, describe the challenges and gifts that came from this circumstance.

Example—Difficult Situation: I lost my father.

Challenges	Gifts
I miss him terribly.	It has caused me to rely more on God.
No one could love me like he did.	I have reached out to others more.
It has created a closer bond with my siblings.	I can relate to others who've gone through this pain.

Difficult Situation:

Challenges	Gifts

6.   What new thoughts do you have about your circumstance after discovering the gifts in the challenge? Write a sentence that shows the gift in the challenge.

You're blessed when you feel you've lost what is most dear to you. Only then can you be embraced by the One most dear to you.

(Matthew 5:4 msg)

The challenges we go through can feel like a handicap until we realize that God can work all things for our good. (See Romans 8:28.)

Look at how Paul views his handicap in this passage:

Because of the extravagance of those revelations, and so I wouldn't get a big head, I was given the gift of a handicap to keep me in constant touch with my limitations. Satan's angel did his best to get me down; what he in fact did was push me to my knees. No danger then of walking around high and mighty! At first I didn't think of it as a gift, and begged God to remove it. Three times I did that, and then he told me,

My grace is enough; it's all you need.

My strength comes into its own in your weakness.

Once I heard that, I was glad to let it happen. I quit focusing on the handicap and began appreciating the gift. It was a case of Christ's strength moving in on my weakness. Now I take limitations in stride, and with good cheer, these limitations that cut me down to size—abuse, accidents, opposition, bad breaks. I just let Christ take over! And so the weaker I get, the stronger I become.   (2 Corinthians 12:7–10 msg)

Paul saw his challenges as a gift. It kept him humble and caused him to rely more on God. By facing the storm, he came to the revelation that God's grace was enough—indeed, all he needed—and he actually began appreciating the gifts that came in the challenge!

Something that is important to remember is that grief is not an unhealthy emotion, and no one else can tell you how long grief should last.

Everyone is different as a result of their story. But Jesus makes it clear in the Beatitudes of Matthew 5 that grief doesn't have to continue to rob us of our happiness and contentment. He says that we're actually "blessed" when difficult things come our way!

> All this trouble is a clear sign that God has decided to make you fit for the kingdom.   (2 Thessalonians 1:5 MSG)

God wants us to deeply understand that "Christ in us" is the only thing that can complete us, satisfy our wants and desires, turn challenges into gifts, and, as Paul says, make us *"fit for the kingdom."*

7. In what areas of your life do you see God moving you towards being *"fit for the kingdom"*?

8. As you become healthier both spiritually and emotionally, how might that improve the relationships with your spouse, your kids, and with your coworkers?

9. As you have come to understand that your worth and value comes from Christ in you, that He is your true identity, and that you no longer have to walk in fear and condemnation, how has that changed your life over the several weeks of this study?

10. Now that you've gone deeper into the wilds, are you ready to do something different with your life? What will that look like?

When a man knows who he is in Christ, that he is created in the image of the living God, that he is no longer held captive by the opinions of others, and that he is no longer afraid of whether he lives or dies, he now knows the dangerous truth that every man needs to know. Now he is fully equipped to go...*Into the Wilds!*

—*Brent Alan Henderson*

THE HOME FRONT

LOVE CONQUERS ALL

Is it not clear to you that to go back to that old rule-keeping,
peer-pleasing religion would be an abandonment of everything
personal and free in my relationship with God? I refuse to do that, to
repudiate God's grace. If a living relationship with God could come by
rule-keeping, then Christ died unnecessarily."
—Apostle Paul (Galatians 2:21 MSG)

I n life, you will constantly be presented with opportunities to live out the things that you've learned along the way. You may have learned these things in the wild, at church, from reading the Bible, from being discipled, or from discipling others. Nevertheless, you have learned them, and you're learning to implement them in your day-to-day life. This is what the Home Front is all about. Trying to explain to men that challenges are gifts, and that accountability doesn't come through extensive to-do lists, will never be an easy task, but with the right gear, experience, knowledge, and faith, and by casting our nets when the Spirit moves us to do so, that explanation will get easier over time. That said, dealing with your own failure and loss, and trying to remain faithful when you get stuck in the moss and mud, will be next to impossible unless you have access to men who know God and are willing to help *guide you through the spiritual wilderness.*

WARNING: As you walk through this spiritual wilderness, *beware* of the voices you're listening to. If they are coming from a place of shame and condemnation, run, don't walk, to the nearest *exit*, and then find a voice that aligns with the gospel of Jesus Christ. Anyone who suggests that **the way to God = Jesus + your own efforts at holiness** is simply spouting heresy—false teaching.

I was on a plane to California a few years ago when I struck up a conversation with a man sitting next to me. He shared with me that his church had recently asked a man to leave their congregation because of a certain sin in his life. They accused the man of refusing to be held accountable by the leadership team for this unhealthy choice he was making. When I asked why the church member was asked to leave, he said, "It was brought to our attention that the man is 'shacked up' with a harlot, and we can't support that. The Bible says that if your brother sins, confront them, then take a witness with you, and then, if they haven't stopped their sinful ways, take it before the church. If they still haven't turned from their wicked behavior, the church must cast them out. The Bible says they should be treated the same as a pagan or tax collector."

Now, let me clarify something. The "sinner" in this story wasn't guilty of breaking a state or federal law; he was "guilty" of living with a woman outside of wedlock. He was refusing to conform to a church practice affixed in biblical teaching. But was his living situation the root of the problem? And does it seem that the leadership of this church was placing different weight on different sins, all the while judging who was welcome in their church and who was not welcome?

The man I was talking to was extremely obese and woofing down a package of cookies as we spoke. This man went on to describe how he was working eighty-plus hours a week in ministry, and how hard that is on your health and on a family. It sure seemed that eating addictions (gluttony) were acceptable in his church. So was being a workaholic.

I asked the man to clarify his statement about what he thought it meant to treat the sinner as a pagan or tax collector.

His said, "I was always taught that it meant to shake the dust off your feet; condemn them and have nothing to do with them. That will change them."

I then asked, "Where is that passage found in the Bible?"

"In Matthew," he replied.

"And what was Matthew?" I asked.

"Well, he was a tax collector."

A puzzled look crossed on his face.

"And how did Jesus treat tax collectors?"

Silence.

After a few moments of reflection, he raised his head and said, "He loved them."

I then asked, "What does the term *"brother"* mean when the passage says, *'If your brother...sins...'?*"

He began to respond, saying, "My fellow man...."

Then his face changed. The term "brother" is usually used in context of either someone who is related through blood or through shared experiences. I then asked him what the man's name was, or if he knew any more about the man they had asked to leave the church.

Again, silence.

If God is truly a "condemning" God, who in this story bears the most condemnation? The man living out of wedlock? The "harlot" who was causing the man to sin? Or the man sitting beside me, who was judging them both even though he didn't know the "sinner's" name, or his story?

The passage the man on the plane referred to is found in Matthew 18, which simply teaches that when a person is not receiving the truth, we are to start over with them. Remain patient with them as you would an unbeliever (pagan), and love them like Jesus loved the tax collector. Jesus spent time with them, He got into their world. That's how Jesus loves us. Any other way of interpreting those verses leaves us feeling that it's our job to fix and control others. This only leaves us frustrated and the "sinner" feeling rejected and condemned. Doesn't sound much like Jesus, does it?

If that man on the plane would have just read a little further in that passage, he would have read that Jesus instructs us to forgive our brother "*not seven times, but seventy-seven times*" (Matthew 18:22). In other words, you don't throw the sinner out; you begin again. "*Remember, they have their own history to deal with. Treat them gently*" (Romans 14:1 MSG).

How powerful would it have been for this man, and his church, to love this couple through their process, and to leave the untangling of lies coming from the enemy to the Holy Spirit's promptings and timing? Walking through the rawness and fires of life together is how a deep, rich community is forged. Love conquers all.

LOVING THROUGH LOSS

Loss is hard. Growing up in a Christian home, I was always taught not to use the word "suck." Well, sometimes there is only one word that truly describes a situation, and pardon my crassness, but loss *sucks*! It leaves you with a gaping wound like being hit with a .470 Nitro Express bullet that has already mushroomed. You keep trying to fill the resulting hole with "stuff," but that never works. The wound remains. No matter how much you try to deny it, ignore it, hide it, or try be positive about it, the wound exists, and it will hold you down until you deal with it. You have to invite Christ into your deepest wounds.

This book is meant to help men find their way through the wilderness, both physically and spiritually. It lays a course for men to follow. The theme of that course: men can't go it alone. Most men default to thinking that it's easier to do things on your own than to ask for help. We think, *That light bulb is not too high. I don't need anyone to hold my ladder. I've got this.*

It's a guy thing. We put a lot of effort into trying to be perfect, but realizing that we aren't perfect can be a bigger step than achieving any state of perfection.

I was hunting a property in Indiana owned by my friend Brandon, who had recently moved away to Colorado. We almost always hunt his land together, and we never hunt an area unless we've first let the other one know exactly where we are, in case of an emergency.

This day was the exception.

Almost two years prior, my parents had been in a terrible car accident. As they sat at a traffic light, they were rear-ended by a young driver going around 50 mph and not paying attention. I was crossing the border from Maine into Canada to speak for a men's retreat. That night drastically altered the course of my life, and it was not a course I wanted to travel. The injuries my father sustained in the crash ended the way my father and I would be able to communicate. It was the end of a ten-year ministry I'd had with him, in which we traveled the world, adventuring and ministering to men. The enemy had gotten his claws into us and brought down a ministry that had already reached tens of thousands of men, and had the potential to reach many more.

I hate the enemy.

As I arrived at the Canadian retreat grounds around midnight, I spent the rest of the night praying and talking with my sister, trying to get details. Mom had broken her leg in the accident, but Dad had sustained brain damage. The following morning, after speaking for the retreat, I was able to get a flight to Florida, where Dad had already gone through surgery. He would spend the better part of the next three months in a coma. My travel schedule was busy that spring, so my wife traveled to Florida, along with my aunt, and spent a month there taking care of my mother while Dad was hospitalized.

Weeks later, I was speaking for another men's retreat in Georgia. Minutes before I was to begin the second session of the day, my phone rang. It was my wife. She said, "Brent, there's someone here who'd like to talk to you." As I listened closely, I could barely make out the sound of a man whispering: "Brent, I love you." It was my father. Tears began pouring down my face. They'd bought a CD player and began playing one of my songs when he came out of the coma. The song title was "No One Speaks Your Name Like Jesus." Jesus was calling his name, and now my father was calling mine!

For the next year, Dad would be moved from hospital to hospital, from rehab facility to rehab facility, and my elderly mother was getting worn out taking care of him. She needed help, and my sister, her family, and other friends and family members all stepped up. Dad could no longer walk, comprehend letters on a page, go to the bathroom on his own, or, for the most part, feed himself. It's a difficult thing to watch a man lose the ability to do even the simplest tasks. It took a toll on everyone, especially Dad. This pillar of a man, the one who took me fishing and hunting, even though it wasn't his thing, was now the one who needed constant help.

This is where the words "it sucked" should be inserted.

Now, two years later, I sat in a tree stand at my friend's deer camp. The sun had just come up, and I was feeling hopeful for the day. Then my cell phone began chirping. It was my sister. "Brent," she said, "Dad's had a massive stroke and they don't think he's going to make it." Strangely enough, it took a couple of hours for the urgency of the situation to sink in. I was in disbelief. I didn't want to face it. I tried to downplay it. I didn't want him to die, and somehow I thought that by ignoring the facts, they would go away. I wasn't ready to be alone a world without my dad.

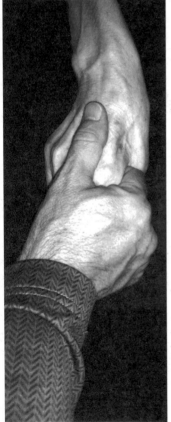

Me holding Dad's hand shortly before he passed away.

Once the cloud in my head cleared, I threw everything in the back of my truck, and drove four hundred miles to be by his bedside. In accordance with family wishes, the medical staff stopped giving Dad food and water. They said he'd probably last two more days. He could not move his arms or legs, couldn't speak, and his mouth was open and drawn. Only his eyes could move, and they were focused on what was most important to him—his family.

Dad wouldn't pass away for another six days, and I spent most of that time swabbing his mouth with a damp cotton swab, holding his hand, singing hymns, and telling stories of all the memories we'd shared together. At times, we'd wonder if he was able to hear us, but then at some point, while retelling a story we'd shared together many times, a tear would run down his cheek. The lights that shone so brightly throughout his life were fading. He could hear us, and he knew he wasn't alone.

The funeral home was packed with people all saying versions of the same thing: "Your dad was the kindest man we've ever known. He never talked about himself, but always made sure to ask about me, my family, my job. He made sure to let you know that you weren't alone."

People stood around way after the viewing, sharing tales of his life. Everyone could feel the power of a shared life and drank it in. A Dietrich Bonhoeffer quote really exemplifies the kind of community my father's love for others created around him:

> The person who loves their dream of community will destroy community, but the person who loves those around them will create community.[8]

For the next four months, Mom went through deep depression. She'd lost her love. She came to stay at our house in Indiana for five weeks, but then decided to live alone at the apartment they had shared, probably because she felt closer to Dad there, even though we all advised her to not live alone. But she was determined.

I was speaking in Iowa when I received a phone call early on a Sunday morning. It was my sister again. "Brent, Mom fell last night in her apartment and broke four ribs. She's at the hospital now but there's no need for you to drive from Iowa to Pennsylvania."

Just before my trip to Iowa, Mom had realized that she couldn't live alone. She planned to return to Indiana and live with her sister, who only lived a block from us. Two weeks after her fall, I received a call from my niece in Pennsylvania. "Uncle Brent," she said, "Nana has developed pneumonia and they're only giving her a couple of weeks to live."

The following morning, my phone rang again. "Uncle Brent, Nana has taken a turn for the worse. It's only going to be hours."

I was out of the house within the hour. Once again, I drove four hundred miles to watch my only remaining parent leave this earth. When I arrived, Mom could no longer talk, but she took my hand as soon as she heard my voice, and kissed it, twice. A few hours later, after she'd been mostly unresponsive, the funniest thing happened: she specifically looked up into the corner of the hospital room and formed the biggest smile I'd ever seen. She hadn't smiled much for the past two years. She was seeing

8. Dietrich Bonhoeffer, *Life Together* (New York: HarperOne, 2009).

something, and she was no longer alone. God was there, calling her by name. Two hours later, she took her final breath.

The following day, after making funeral arrangements and picking out flower arrangements, I drove to the Pittsburgh area to speak for a men's wild beast feast. After checking into my hotel room, I closed the shades and, like a dam bursting, it all spilled out. All the grieving I'd been holding back from Dad's passing, to the raw emotions of witnessing Mom's home-coming, came out in a hot mess. And I was alone in my hotel room.

After not being able to get the images of her final breath and fixed eyes out of my head, I sat up in bed and said aloud, "God, I can't do this alone anymore. I need You to show up!"

Instantly, I felt the Holy Spirit say, "I'm here, and I'm going to show you something that will bring you peace and comfort. Brent, the moment your mother took her last breath and her eyes fixed, they were fixed on something you can't even dream or imagine. Everything has been made new. She's not alone, and never has been alone. She can see that now."

I can't even find the words to express what happened in me at that moment. I knew Mom wasn't alone, but God also revealed to me that I wasn't alone either.

Here are a couple of lines from the song that woke Dad up from his coma:

In my darkness, Jesus came to rescue me,
Just like Lazarus, He called my name
And now I'm free…forever free!

I was beginning to understand that I was no longer alone, but God would remind me that in this life, I would continue to face trials. He wanted me to develop a band of brothers that I could reach out to, walk with, and pray with. He reminded me that I have friends and family who have been with me through all the storms and shipwrecks, people who love me and have taught me so much about myself. I have two beautiful children, Garrett and Emma, who are truly gifts from God that I have been entrusted with to raise and love. A mentor was given to me in Derek; a pastor was given to me in Chris; a life coach in Brandon; and many brothers in Christ have been found along my journey.

But, even if all that were taken away tomorrow, I knew I would be okay, because my security is found in Christ alone. I never have to be alone again. I no longer need to wear just the "hat and T-shirt," but I am clothed in righteousness. I have everything I will ever need...forever.

No one speaks your name like Jesus
No one feels your pain like He does
Even in your darkest hour
He'll find you there
With only a word your deepest sorrow
Can become a bright tomorrow
For no one speaks your name
Like Jesus

—"No One Speaks Your Name" by Brent Henderson

Brent and a 535-pound wild boar.

Brent and his Safari Club International record book impala.

An Indiana buck with Bear Archery.

A large Ohio buck from 2013.

In a boat full of bucks with my friend Wade.

Southern Indiana gobbler with 1¾-inch spurs.

Brent and Stacy Henderson

ABOUT THE AUTHOR

Brent Alan Henderson is the executive director of MenMinistry.org and a nationwide speaker, author, professional outdoorsman and ordained men's ministry pastor. He's been featured at hundreds of outreach events, including the Billy Graham Crusade and Promise Keepers. Brent speaks at over forty events per year, including men's retreats, seminars, wild game dinners, and men's leadership conferences. Brent is also a national recording artist, having toured with Dove and Grammy Award-winning artists, including Steven Curtis Chapman, Sandi Patti, Avalon, and Crystal Lewis. His passion is blending transformational teaching through the lens of Scripture and the wilds of nature to awaken a man's core and help him discover who he is in Christ.

For booking information go to: www.brentalanhenderson.com

Welcome to Our House!

We Have a Special Gift for You

It is our privilege and pleasure to share in your love of Christian books. We are committed to bringing you authors and books that feed, challenge, and enrich your faith.

To show our appreciation, we invite you to sign up to receive a specially selected **Reader Appreciation Gift**, with our compliments. Just go to the Web address at the bottom of this page.

God bless you as you seek a deeper walk with Him!

WE HAVE A GIFT FOR YOU. VISIT:

whpub.me/nonfictionthx

WHITAKER
HOUSE